Lynn Garlick holds a Doctorate of Creative Arts and has lectured in writing and journalism. She has extensive experience as a social worker and educator. She is an experienced writer and arts magazine editor. Her autobiographical work has been published in *The Sydney Morning Herald* and *Griffith Review*. *Binding: More than a Motherhood Memoir* is her first book.

Binding

More Than a Motherhood Memoir

Lynn Garlick

First published by Ten Mothers Publishing in 2022
This edition published in 2022 by Ten Mothers Publishing

Copyright © Lynn Garlick 2022
www.lynngarlick.com.au
The moral right of the author has been asserted.

All rights reserved. This publication (or any part of it) may not be reproduced or transmitted, copied, stored, distributed or otherwise made available by any person or entity (including Google, Amazon or similar organisations), in any form (electronic, digital, optical, mechanical) or by any means (photocopying, recording, scanning or otherwise) without prior written permission from the publisher.

Binding

EPUB: 9781922389756
POD: 9781922389763

Cover design by Red Tally Studios

Publishing services provided by Critical Mass
www.critmassconsulting.com

For my mother and my daughters

Contents

Prologue	1
KNOTS	7
Not Quite the Beginning	9
Honouring the Married and Fertile	12
Neither Past nor Future	18
The Getting of Wisdom	27
Wonder-Watching	37
Attachment	42
The Surprise of not Being Stable	49
Journey of a New Planet Earth Dweller	55
Olivia	63
Fight or Flight	72
Memorial for the Common Man	79
DUCT TAPE	87
Why?	89
Duct Tape for the Soul	96
The Positivity of Americans	101
Verbraekennisation	107

The Happiest Place on Earth	117
Entrapment	124
Bound	131
BRAIDING	**143**
The Return	145
Elaborate Covers	150
Snow Dome	158
My Situation	168
Pirates	176
Divorce Night Jitters	185
Creating a New Story	191
Bronfenbrenner's Babushkas	197
Broken Homes	202
The Year of Upside Downs	210
Work/Life Wheel	220
Paris with Loner Issues	232
At the Pantheon with the Obamas	243
Shifting	255
Teenagers Tear at One's Bowel	259
Epilogue	267
Author's Note	271
Acknowledgements	273

Prologue

I could hear my baby crying as I ran past the university library, heading towards the strictly fifteen-minute parking bays where I could see our car parked with the back doors open. I ran with my arms crossed in front of my chest, trying to maintain an aura of professionalism, while also trying to still my hot and heavy breasts that had been filling all morning and now threatened to burst their maternity bra restraints. The Coles shopping bag I was clutching swung from side to side with my body's movement; it held fifty-six student assignments. I saw Sonia escape the car and run towards me, calling, 'Mummy, Mummy.' I didn't bend down to hug her, as I needed to reach the car as soon as possible and I didn't want her to come into contact with my breasts, which felt as solid as bricks. So, when we met, she hugged my knees, nearly tackling me. I gave her my free hand and we ran together to the car.

'I love you, Mummy.'

'I love you too, Sonia.'

We continued to run along together.

'Mummy, I got McDonald's.'

'Did you?'

When I opened the front car door, I caught the whiff of a McDonald's Happy Meal, so it's possible my face might not have looked as friendly as I had intended when I greeted my husband, Andrew. My face might also have shown surprise that Andrew's hair was blond, which it wasn't when I left the house. Dying his hair was something he had only started doing since he became a father. It took my attention for a moment and I wondered how he had managed to do that while caring for a two-month-old and a two-year-old. Most days I was lucky to have time to shower. A shower where I actually had the time to get the mix of hot and cold water just right was a distant memory.

'Bit late!' he said loudly over the crying. He passed Olivia to me like a football.

'Sorry. A student needed help with an assignment.'

I held Olivia as I flipped the lever, shooting the front seat back, unlooped the bright cotton scarf around my neck, hooked it over my shoulder to drape as a makeshift cover and hoicked up my black dress. I popped open the flesh-coloured maternity bra cup to expose a plump breast.

Olivia latched on; I flinched. Mastitis had burned red infected patches across my breasts in the shape of Italy and France. The doctor had assured me the milk itself was not infected and that the only way to relieve the pain was to get the milk out. Olivia wanted and needed the milk, but the pain made her little mouth feel like a cheese grater on my nipple. Olivia kicked her legs and huffed and groaned. I wiped the soft tears that barely wet her face. 'It's alright,' I said as I stroked her light brown hair. Then she looked up at me, as if to check I was really the one that feeds her. She turned her head back and I tensed in anticipation as she brought down the cheese grater again.

'Did she drink the milk I expressed?'

'Wouldn't take it.'

'Oh, poor baby, no wonder she's hungry.'

Feeding Olivia in our car in the university car park had not been the plan. I didn't have maternity leave when she was born because I'd left my permanent role as a manager in a public health service after Sonia's birth. My workplace hadn't allowed me to work part time after my maternity leave ended. The CEO at the time could not conceive of a manager role being a job share arrangement, so I didn't return and instead, I took on casual work at a university. For seven hours on Thursdays I delivered a lecture at nine am, followed by three two-hour tutorials. This arrangement allowed me to earn a decent income for only a day away from my children, as most preparation, marking and communication with students was completed at home. As a casual lecturer I had no access to an office where I could work, meet with students or breastfeed with privacy. The university prayer room had been suggested as a place to breastfeed. I didn't take up that offer. So, every Thursday during my lunch break, Andrew drove to the university and we sat as a family in the car park while Sonia ate in the backseat and I breastfed in the front seat. I was more fortunate in this arrangement than one of my colleagues, who brought a breast pump and insulated bag and bottles with her to work each day to express milk in the Ladies toilet.

During the rest of the week, I taught at TAFE and took on project work as a consultant, because I could do that from home too. I'd work at night when the children slept. I might work through to two am, then rise again at six to breastfeed, then sleep in the middle of the day when Sonia and Olivia napped. This combination of work and family in the home could be managed swimmingly if everyone went to sleep on schedule. Unfortunately, our baby and toddler had not signed on to the contract.

Andrew worked weekends, but not Wednesdays and Thursdays, so that's when I worked outside the home. One of us, Andrew or myself, would clock on for our childcare duty as the other clocked off. We enacted this tag-teaming with high fives, when we had the energy and good will. This arrangement meant we didn't need to pay for childcare; the downside was that we no longer spent time as a couple, or a family. The teamwork had dropped at nights, however, with Andrew coming home from work later and later, so there was no one to help me with the feeding, bathing, reading, cuddling and lullabying routine.

Sonia was standing on the floor in the back of the car, leaning through to the front to entertain Olivia with the plastic yellow and red clock that Grandma had given to her. It went *klklklklkl* as she turned the hands, and *tringgg, tringgg* when the hands reached the hour – the type of toy that only a grandmother could give a child. It offered visual, auditory and kinaesthetic stimulation in a compact shape, so it was Sonia's 'go-to toy'. It helped her to direct attention away from the new imposter in her life. Sonia sped up time, turning the dial in nonstop revolutions, *tringgg, tringgg, tringgg*. Olivia lifted her head dreamily in response to the noises, sending a dribble of milk running down the side of her mouth. Then she'd remember what she was doing and purposefully latch on again as I tensed with the pain.

I turned to Andrew, who was reading *The Sydney Morning Herald*.

'Can you take Sonia outside to play?'

Prologue

'Why?'

'She's disturbing Olivia.'

'Where would we play – in the car park?'

'Oh, never mind.'

Olivia lifted her head again, exposing my breast just at the moment a group of students passed the car. If they had seen the scene inside the car, I was curious as to how they might interpret it. I was reminded of the famous painting, *Liberty Leading the People* by Delacroix, in which Liberty, also with one breast exposed is holding a French flag in one hand and a gun in the other. She is the symbol of a revolution, leading the people in the painting out of tyranny to a better future. I similarly momentarily had a breast exposed but in my hands was a baby. The man next to me was reading the paper and the child behind me was eating fast food. The students, if they had actually seen inside the car, would have no way of knowing that, like Liberty, I too was leading a revolutionary movement. Unlike Liberty's, my revolution was a personal and silent one, which had begun since having children, moving me from 'self-full' to selfless, professional to profession-less, full time to casual, independent to dependent.

Still feeding Olivia, I turned my head to where Sonia was playing in the back of the car and I smiled at her. She held my face with her greasy chicken-nugget fingers, locking my twisted neck in this uncomfortable position to plant a loud kiss on my cheek. Then she opened my mouth and placed a cold and dried up chip inside.

*

The author Giulia Giuffrè in her book about raising her children, *Primavera*, offers the Sicilian expression, '*figli nigli*', to explain the unique mix of joy and pain in being a parent. She writes that '*Figli*' suggests enjoying the nurturing, while '*nigli*' loosely translates as 'being simultaneously eaten alive by birds of prey'.

KNOTS

Not Quite the Beginning

Nothing made me more focused on having a child than being told in my twenties that I might never have one.

I remember the awkward silence in the examination room, but I don't remember any distinguishing features of the gynaecologist himself, because I made as little eye contact as possible. Sharp pains that struck randomly in what I assumed were my ovaries had led to the appointment at the Macquarie Street establishment. My doctor had said this gynaecologist was the best in Sydney. I also avoided looking at the metal instruments in kidney-shaped trays while I was lying on the examination table. I did this by looking at the walls and their framed art prints of fertile flowers – flowers the size of landscapes. My gaze was drawn inside the vibrant folds of red canna lilies, sensual curves of black irises and soft budding sweet peas. They were Georgia O'Keefe prints.

I wiped away the excess gel from my thighs and pulled my clothes back on. I didn't know what to do with the hospital gown. Fold it or leave it scrunched? I left it scrunched, then walked out from behind the screen to find the gynaecologist assessing my ultrasound images. They appeared over a large light box at eye height and looked like moonscapes. Black and white, smooth and round. When he saw me, he gathered the images from the light box, slid them into a large white envelope and placed them on his desk. He invited me to sit on the opposite side of the large solid oak table. As he spoke, he drew on the corner of the envelope with a silver ballpoint pen. He drew meticulous little circles that touched at their outer edges and looked like fish eggs, just a teaspoonful. On other days, for other women, he might have drawn well-formed circles to represent the first cells of life, but the circles he drew for me represented something else. I watched his ballpoint circling. Then he impassively dropped the word bomb – infertile. My hands quickly moved to cover my belly as if I'd been kicked in the guts.

By the time I settled the account with the receptionist my sunglasses were already pressed into the service of hiding my tearful eyes. She looked up when I sniffled. This seemed to spark a curiosity in her. She examined my credit card assiduously before taking her time with the payment. Her manner suggested to me that the manila folder with my name on it might accidentally fall open and she would stamp the word 'infertile' in red at an angle across it.

I pushed open the heavy glass door and found myself swept up in the purposeful movement of the lunchtime crowd in Martin Place. I just wanted a taxi to drive me home, but I couldn't have provided a destination. I felt directionless and couldn't speak. At that moment, a memory of the paintings and sculptures of Mary and the baby Jesus I'd seen in galleries returned to me. When I'd travelled in Europe a few years earlier, I'd been moved by these artworks, not so much for their religious significance, but because they captured the emotion of a lifetime of connection between a mother and a child. Reuben's painting of a mother breastfeeding and Botticelli's painting of a mother besotted with her son, the sadness in Lippi's painting of a mother who holds her chubby baby protectively because she knows his fate. In Egypt, too, I remembered the ancient statues of the powerful goddess Isis, who wore a sun disk and cow horns on her head as she sat breastfeeding her son. Each image flashed through my mind, like flicking through the pages of a thick coffee table art book.

When I realised I had passed the train station entrance, I turned and retraced my steps, head down, consciously placing one foot in front of the other and that's why I couldn't anticipate the oncoming pram before it rammed into my legs. When I looked up, I saw a toddler inside the pram, then I saw that Martin Place was filled with children. Happy children running, splashing the fountain water, talented children performing on the stage of the amphitheatre. I was surrounded by a wild jamboree that screeched a high-pitched anarchy. I had no reason to remember that it was school holidays. As I increased my pace, paintings and sculptures of mother and child morphed in my head with the mothers in suits around me feeding their children sushi or Vegemite sandwiches. In Martin Place at lunchtime, in Europe or Egypt, there was no evading the mystery and potency of mothers and their children.

I escaped into the silent underground station made void of life by the exiting train. On the platform, I stared at the blackness between the metal tracks, both hands resting on my belly as more images flashed through my mind. Georgia O'Keefe's artworks appeared in my mind again, not the fertile budding flower paintings that hung from the gynaecologist's walls, but the paintings I had forgotten she had also painted – the barren desert landscapes.

Honouring the Married and Fertile

I did not tell anybody about the visit to the gynaecologist, especially my family. Gynaecology was not something my family discussed. Mum and Dad were solid double-brick-type people. Stable, reliable, dependable. They always appeared as a happy couple. In fact, as a child I felt so secure in my family, that when I soaked in my warm bath each night, staring at the patterns in the leadlight windows, I wondered how other children could get through life without my mum and dad as their parents.

As a child, our meals were eaten with the five of us cosied up on benches in a 1950's original kitchen nook where we laughed a lot. I see in photos taken from that time that our kitchen was small and made smaller by the choice of brightly patterned wallpaper. Behind the kitchen door, hanging with the dog's lead that jangled with the opening and closing, was Dad's brown leather belt. While eating Froot Loops for breakfast, we could see this instrument of discipline suspended threateningly from its silver buckle. The sight of Dad's belt each time the kitchen door closed was enough to keep the three of us in line, at least until we were older. When my brother grew as tall as Dad he was given a lot of freedoms, but he also 'got the belt' a lot. As I started to grow as tall as my mum I wasn't given the same freedoms as my brother. I also 'got the belt', but only once. I was thirteen when it happened. The belt wrapped around my legs and the prong of the buckle pierced a finger and ripped off skin. To this day, I don't understand what I did to deserve it, and despite Dad's assurances that the belt would 'teach me a lesson', it didn't. But it did change my relationship with my father. Afterwards, I began to fantasise about how great it would be if my friends' parents were my mum and dad instead. Years later, when we were parents ourselves, my childhood friend since kindergarten, Nicola revealed that when I had been wishing to be part of her family, she had been wishing for mine.

Around the timing of the belt incident, I became aware of the way my parents divided the world into two types of people: those who were 'smart in practical ways that got you by in life' and 'those who only knew things in books and had no common sense'. As someone who loved to read and liked school, it left me with a difficult choice. My parents wanted me to leave school in Year 10 to do something 'practical'. They expected that I would complete a TAFE qualification as they had done and my siblings had done. Many girls at my school left at the end of Year 10. One day when I was walking to the science labs, the dux of our year, Maria Dimi, casually asked what I was planning to study at university. That was all it took for me to see myself in a new way, the way that the smartest girl saw me, as an inevitable university student. Back home, my father made it clear that if I was to finish high school, he would not support me. My mother didn't challenge him. But in my bedroom that night, she saw how it had upset me and said to me that I should do whatever I wanted.

When she could, our neighbour, Mrs Randall, would weigh in with her opinion: 'Why would you want to go to university when you'll only marry and have kids?' This baffled me because Mrs Randall was married but didn't have children.

I continued on to Year 12. I set a goal to go to university, but had no idea what to study. At a careers market I collected pamphlets about every career possible. One that struck me read, 'Social workers are not starry-eyed do-gooders'. I thought it odd to promote a profession by what it was not, rather than clarifying what it was, but the pamphlet did spark my curiosity. I asked the straight-backed woman handing out the pamphlets, 'What do social workers do?'

'Social workers help the vulnerable, they fight for justice and they improve lives.'

She made social workers sound like kick-ass superheros, a bit like my grandmother, who I greatly admired, so after the HSC, I enrolled to become one.

Being the first person to go to university from my family afforded me an unusual status. My father, brother and brother-in-law made jokes at dinner time that continued to build on the theme of how people at university only knew things in books and had no common sense. One would start and the other would pick up on that theme. The women around the table would stay silent or laugh along as I also had to. I received the message loud and clear that I was now seen as different by my family. I wished that I had the money to move out and house share in the inner city like my peers.

Eventually, I started to retaliate. I began to lob my newly gained 'book knowledge' back at them. I'd impart a critique of 'the patriarchal hegemony that existed within our residence' while we ate Mum's apricot chicken and it continued until the apple pie and ice cream was served. Then I'd leave my plate on the sink for Mum to wash. I'd return to my bedroom to read the feminist texts I'd been assigned.

*

We studied families in social work, but nothing we learned helped me to deal with this situation in my own. Oddly, the first thing we learned about families in my social work degree was how to draw them, not as stick figures, but as shapes on genograms. Like a family tree, a genogram can summarise a family's story and connections. A genogram can save the family repeating that story to different helping professionals, because one look at a genogram by a trained eye can reveal a family's structure, their dynamics and even their secrets. In the genogram, circles represent females, squares represent males and rhombuses are gender-neutral. The lines connecting these shapes show the quality of the relationship. Some lines are straight and solid, some quiver and shake, some are dotted or cut.

My own family genogram at that time would be represented by Dad's square attached to Mum's circle by a solid straight line, the date of their marriage proudly inscribed above it in permanent ink. Descending from that line, a square and two circles would represent my brother, sister and me. Years after I finished university, my siblings, both older than me, were each connected to a partner, and my nieces and nephews, as four circles and two squares, would crowd the space below them. It made the silence of the white space around me even louder. My circle hung from the family genogram like a forgotten bauble left dangling on the

Christmas tree long after the other baubles had been packed away.

My parents had their own way of representing their family. It only honoured the married and fertile, although I'm sure this was an unconscious bias. In the lounge room above the fireplace, Mum had covered the mantelpiece with a length of intricate needlework. Across the multi-coloured tapestry – a symbolically fitting platform for people coming together – she had lovingly placed framed photographs of my siblings' weddings. As each new grandchild arrived their photographs were proudly added, eventually eclipsing the wedding photos that were pushed further to the back.

As I was not married and did not have a child, I was the only member of the family not to appear in a photograph in the lounge room. I was however in a photograph on a wall in the sunroom. Locked inside a thin aluminium frame, I was perpetually five years old. The sun-bleached photograph showed my freckle-specked face with what Dad called 'wing nut' ears peeking out either side of two long blonde plaits. A wide smile revealed two missing teeth. Draped over me was an oversized blue school uniform, sewn by my mother – the way Mum sewed all my clothes, 'for growth'. The uniform is pressed into straightness for the first day of school and hangs like the triangle symbol for females used on toilet doors. I suggested to Mum that perhaps the school photograph could be replaced by the photograph taken at my university graduation. This move would suggest to visitors that although I wasn't married or had children, I, like my brother and sister, did adult things. Despite their earlier misgivings about me furthering my studies, my parents came around and supported my education and were very proud when I graduated. Mum listened to my suggestion and on my next visit, my graduation photograph was displayed, but it didn't replace my yellowing kindergarten photo that remained in the sunroom. My graduation photograph joined the 'celebration of the married and fertile family' on the mantelpiece. Each time I passed through the lounge room, I came face to face with a younger version of myself striding confidently from a sandstone building across a manicured lawn. I was dressed in black robes, balancing a black mortarboard on my head, next to my sister and sister-in-law, both dressed in white, balancing glistening tiaras and veils on their heads. I held a piece of paper. They each held a husband. When my photograph was placed next to that of my siblings in this way, I imagine my family saw me as the consolation prize winner.

Certainly, relatives judged this photograph as a sign of defeat, because at birthdays, weddings and funerals, aunts, uncles and cousins who used to greet me with, 'How's your love life?' began to ask, 'How's work?'

Neither Past nor Future

My graduation photograph remained an imposter on the tapestry that honoured the married and fertile until I legitimately made my way onto the tapestry in an ivory-hued, lace-and-silk, halter-necked wedding dress.

I had met Andrew at a mutual friend's 21st birthday party in Brisbane. He was tall, confident and charming. His smile was so lavish that when it arrived his butterscotch eyes almost disappeared. He had an acerbic wit, imitated accents with precision and was quick with a pun. He had studied science at university and had a keen interest in palaeontology. He had just returned from a year overseas that involved some time searching for fossils from the black volcanic mountains of Yemen to the Gobi desert bad lands. He animated his suspenseful survival tales with flash floods, snakes, scorpions and bandits. He was so beguiling that he made me feel I had his total attention, even when he was entertaining the entire party. I bathed in the warm, deep timbre of his voice. We stayed in touch, but it was six years later, when he had come to Sydney for a visit, that we met again. An interstate relationship began, where I often travelled to Brisbane to see him. He was working casual jobs and house-sharing, and spent his nights at the local pub with mates, watching bands and comedy shows. His easy-going lifestyle seemed an enviable contrast to my serious, responsible one. I had a management role in a mental health service and a mortgage on an apartment.

That summer, he arrived at my door with all his belongings in his car. There had been no discussion about him moving and definitely no discussion about him moving in. He said he was missing me, so he had decided to quit his work and come to Sydney. I took this as a significant sign of his commitment. He asked to stay at my house for two weeks until he could find a place to live. He never did look for a place to rent and he never moved out. He was fun to be around and he brought out a carefree quality in me, that made me forget all the boundaries I had previously set for myself in relationships. I supported him financially while he applied for jobs and took on casual work. We both enrolled in Masters programs and worked on them at night after work. Over the next few years when we lived and travelled together, I enjoyed his explications of rock formations, weather patterns and indigenous biota, imparted in the unlikeliest of places – on the side of an active volcano in Guatemala or on horseback in Costa Rica.

*

Over time, the shapes on the family genogram shuffled to allow for Andrew's square to connect to my circle by a line with the date of our marriage written across the top. Our wedding photo muscled its way to the front of the mantel that honoured the married and fertile. In that photo I was suspended in the arms of my husband, while he stood on a sandstone cliff above the glistening Pacific Ocean crashing below. I suppose the photo was meant to symbolise that he had swept me off my feet. To me the photo also symbolised that our marriage would be solid as a rock and that Andrew would be strong and stable. Being assigned a place on the mantel surely bestowed a form of assurance and protection. So, despite knowing that one in three marriages end in divorce, I assumed we would remain bound together forever, like the other smiling couples surrounding us. And despite the meticulous little circles drawn by the gynaecologist, I hoped photographs of our children could also be placed there.

*

Then it happened. I fell pregnant. As easy as that. When our doctor confirmed it, I was holding Andrew's hand. I felt his palm go clammy and saw his face pale. This worried the doctor so much that Andrew was offered a jellybean from the jar stocked for freshly immunised toddlers and diabetics. Andrew's reaction worried me too.

When he recovered, I held his clammy hands as we watched our doctor hold two cardboard circles between his hygienic fingers. The smaller circle, joined to the larger by a small rivet, spun to match with numbers underneath. These were the doctor's tools to calculate forty weeks from the date of the last period. One cardboard circle scraped over the other as he turned it to reveal the months and days underneath. I squeezed Andrew's hand without taking my eyes from the circles as we waited. It felt like I was a child at the community fair waiting for the Lion's Club wheel to stop turning, checking the number on my thin papery ticket, then looking back at the wooden wheel with its rudimentary rubber prongs that *tacktacktacktacked* against the nails as I willed it to stop on the number that matched my ticket. Not that I was actually gunning for one date over another; we were having a baby, what did the date matter? I had thought it would be my body, or the baby itself that determined when they would enter the world, but the way the doctor announced the date with such certainty made it clear that only the doctor and his calculating circles sponsored by a pregnancy supplement called Elevit knew what was happening inside me. Already the doctor was about to set our embryonic mystery to a timer.

'Your baby is due April first – April Fool's Day.'

*

I watched over the months as my bellybutton disappeared down a tunnel only to find it greet me again when it popped out months later. I began to focus on my body in a way I hadn't before and so did strangers, even at professional conferences. This new attention was both appealing and annoying, like being smiled at every time you speak when travelling in America, because of your Australian accent. Despite feeling incredibly sensual in my newfound buxomness, I had to support my recently acquired, oversized bosom in soft-pink or flesh-coloured maternity bras. These had four fasteners at the back, instead of two.

I'd asked to see photos of my mum and Andrew's mum when they were pregnant, but they had none. In their day a pregnancy was something you had to hide for fear of losing your job. When they were working, one in a bank and the other in an office, they were forced to leave their jobs when they married or became pregnant. This seemed like such an ancient concept, but I remembered it wasn't until I was at university that the Anti-Discrimination legislation was introduced, making it illegal for the first time for employers to discriminate against women on the basis of their gender, being married or pregnant.

Before my workplace knew I was pregnant I'd been offered the opportunity to participate in a leadership program as a fast track to an executive position. I didn't consider taking it as it required a number of placements in locations that were up to two hours' drive away. I couldn't see how I could do that with a new baby. Later, when I was able and would have jumped at the chance, I was never offered anything like that opportunity again.

Instead of a focus on career, my focus moved inwards. I felt I had known our cashew-sized embryo even before the ultrasound brought our baby to life as an astronaut enjoying anti-gravity in footage as surreal as a black-and-white moon landing. The ultrasound visit showed our baby hiccupping, spine arching, arm stretching. I watched in silence, mesmerised as all four chambers of the heart beat as flecks of white, appearing and disappearing from the screen. I realised that my connection with the baby was already so different to Andrew's. I felt that he was just catching up with the reality of our situation, whereas I'd been living it. He bombarded the radiologist with questions:

'What's the lateral and temporal resolution?'

'Are the organs functioning?'

"What will grow next?"

A natural delivery in the local hospital's birth centre was our plan. Mostly because fathers could sleep there with their family and bond with the baby immediately, instead of being separated straight after the birth as they did on the wards. This choice also kept us clear of unnecessary intervention, but remained inside the hospital if there was any emergency. The midwife who ran the birth centre was a colleague I greatly admired and trusted and wanted to deliver my baby.

In thinking about how we might raise our child, Andrew and I reflected on how we were raised ourselves. Andrew's father seemed to have been more involved in his family than mine, particularly in cooking meals. I took this as good sign. Andrew was planning to be the main caregiver when I returned to work after maternity leave. It made sense as I had a permanent role with a good salary and he planned to be actively involved in Sonia's life. He seemed to have a natural affinity with children. At family parties he entertained nieces and nephews when the rest of us tended to sit around eating and drinking. It was comforting to know that our relationship would be more equal than how I saw my parents' relationship.

In the final months of the pregnancy, in antenatal classes, we sat in a circle – male, female, male, female, male, female, female, female – as the nurse facilitator asked each set of soon-to-be parents to describe their experience of pregnancy so far. Although each response was different, the group was connecting through their common experiences.

'I hadn't expected how exhausted I would be,' was my offering. The women around the room agreed. We joked about wanting to nod off in boring meetings and napping under desks at work.

Then it was Andrew's turn.

'I wasn't aware that pregnant women could be so moody.'

This elicited laughter and agreement from the soon-to-be dads.

'You're a brave man to say that,' one of the men said and they laughed again. I laughed along, but I didn't think Andrew brave at all.

At the tea break, questions were going through my head: if he thought I was moody, why hadn't he discussed this with me at home? Why did he share this information with a new group of people we would be raising our children with? Did he mean to publicly humiliate me? Was I moody? Was I being too sensitive?

My searching for answers to Andrew's behaviour rather than focusing on socialising at morning tea might have reinforced to the group Andrew's assessment that I was moody. Andrew, however, was as affable as ever, smiling and laughing with the group. His statement had given him a sort of 'bad boy' notoriety amongst the group that he seemed to revel in.

*

In the final months of my pregnancy, my only remaining grandparent had apparently slipped away effortlessly, and I hoped it was true. Dad tried to inform me of her death, holding back tears by tensing his mouth and eyes to the point where he was unable to speak, so I had to guess at the cause. The contortions scored across his face showed the pain of losing a mother.

I gave the eulogy at Nanna's funeral, conscious of my tall, pregnant body standing next to her small, elegant coffin. The heady scent of lilies reminded me of Nanna's garden and made the childhood memories I shared in the eulogy come alive again. I recalled Nanna, sitting on a cushioned seat to patiently braid my hair before bed when my sister, brother and I slept at her house. I'd excitedly position myself on the carpet, cross-legged in front of her chair, and stretch my spine to sit upright in anticipation. She'd smell of roses. Nanna would gently bow my head to begin the bedtime ritual. She'd split my long hair into two sections, using only her pinkie finger down the centre of my scalp, then the weight of half my hair flopped over one shoulder. I'd settle in, lifting my eyes, without lifting my head, to follow the repeated patterns along the floral carpet.

The brush caressed my hair, feeling slowly through the strands for the tug of any knots. Each knot disintegrated under her assertive brushing. Then she'd fold the hair in on itself, weaving an ordered pattern, taking care not to leave any strays. I'd remain still, but tilt my head obediently in the direction it was moved. Sometimes as my head was tilted forward, I caught a glimpse of the varicose veins on her legs like bluebottles on a stretch of sand. I wanted to ask her questions, but didn't. It was a ritual performed in silence.

When I was about eight, my hair had grown down to the dimples in my back and knots often formed under collars that escaped my mother's attention and were hard for me to reach to remove. Nanna always saw in my knotty hair the potential for something strong and beautiful, and she'd easily fashioned it into a new shape. I could watch her life-worn hands dexterously moving like knitting needles through my hair. She kept going with such dedication until the hair naturally ended. She didn't need hair bands or elastics to tie my hair in place; she somehow bound my hair together without additional resources. She'd give my shoulders a hearty squeeze to confirm the ritual had ended. I'd slide my fingers over the smooth crests. When I looked in the mirror, I saw the darker hair that usually hid below collars had mingled with the sun-licked strands, forming a multi-coloured weave.

In the eulogy I used the braiding as an analogy for the way Nanna integrated helping family, friends and community, whether living in a country town or the suburbs of Sydney.

As a community leader, she bound people together. Just like Nanna's unpaid work, binding for me best describes what social workers can do too. They help people pull themselves back together when they feel they are coming unstuck, they can help couples and families to reconnect and they can help to build cohesion in communities.

As I delivered the eulogy next to Nanna's coffin, the tiny life tightening inside me pressed a foot against its cocoon. I laid the palm of my right hand over the camber of the heel. My left hand searched for, and gratefully found, Andrew's right hand beside me.

The Getting of Wisdom

I'd planned to keep working until April Fool's Day, trying to finish projects before the birth. As well as my managerial role, I continued to study for my Masters degree on Monday and Wednesday nights. I taught welfare studies at TAFE on Tuesday nights, I was learning Spanish on Thursday nights, and editing a documentary on weekends. For some reason I didn't understand at the time, my blood pressure spiked three weeks before the baby was due. I developed borderline preeclampsia and was monitored daily in hospital. I spent my thirtieth birthday with other heavily pregnant women with swollen feet and hands sitting along the wall of a small hospital ward like battery hens. Over four hours, nurses tested our blood, urine and blood pressure on a rigid schedule. If anyone's condition worsened, they would be admitted to hospital. I had things I wanted to finish at work and it frustrated me to spend days delivering urine samples instead of delivering outcomes, but when the nurses wrapped the heart monitor across my belly and I heard the loud whooshing watery sound of my baby's heartbeat I was spellbound. The baby's heartbeat was not soft and fragile, as expected, but strong and booming. Those extraordinary sounds grounded me to the chair and focused my attention solely on the mysterious life inside.

I failed some of my battery hen tests, so with the due date still two weeks away I was admitted to hospital to be more intensely monitored. During one of those days confined to the labour ward, Andrew entered through the curtains that arced around my bed. He was smiling and holding a paper bag as if he'd won something.

'Look what I bought you.'

He left the curtains open and I could see the woman in the bed next to me leaning forward to see what it was.

The bag clearly held magazines and I was grateful for something new to read. As I pulled the magazines from the bag, I expected to see a 'yummy mummy' on the cover of a parenting magazine. Instead, it was an African elephant standing in front of Victoria Falls.

'Travel magazines?' I asked, looking up at him from the bed.

'Africa!'

'But we're having a baby? I don't think we'll be...'

I was interrupted by a tall, balding doctor and four younger doctors entering the room. They positioned themselves around the bed, leaving Andrew to vacate to a plastic chair on the opposite side. The doctor at the centre introduced himself as the hospital obstetrician, Dr Jackson. He didn't introduce the other four doctors, who I assumed were registrars. He stretched a rubber glove over the back of his hand, leaving some black hairs peeping above the wrist. He directed a registrar to close the curtains and asked me to open my legs.

'Mmm, your cervix feels like a carrot!'

While still holding my legs apart, he turned to the registrars and asked, 'Would anyone else like to feel it?'

I turned to face Andrew, my eyes wide. Fortunately, the registrars weren't interested.

Dr Jackson then flicked off the rubber glove. He placed one foot on the metal bin at the end of the bed to flip the lid. Then, as if shooting hoops, the glove landed straight in without touching the sides.

'We need to get this baby out.'

He turned back and looked at my face for the first time.

'We'll schedule you for a prostaglandin gel tonight; you'll have your baby in the morning and your blood pressure will return to normal.'

He turned to exit.

I closed my legs and quickly pulled the sheet over them. As the doctor opened the curtains, the metal rings scraped against the metal bar, drowning out my words, so I had to repeat them.

'If I'm not putting my baby at risk and I'm not putting myself at risk, I'd like to try for a natural delivery in the birth centre as planned.'

The specialist turned and walked back towards me. He nearly tripped on my overnight bag, still unpacked in the belief that I would deliver in the birth centre. He moved to sit close to me on the bed. I tried to shift my egg-shaped body sideways in the bedclothes, but didn't make it in time, so I was imprisoned in my sheet close enough to him that I could smell his morning coffee.

'I've read that intervention often leads to more intervention. The breaking of the waters, an epidural, a caesarean...'

'I know every woman wants an easy natural delivery, just like every woman wants thin thighs, but nature just doesn't work that way.'

He tapped the outside of my thighs through the sheets as if to emphasise his point. I felt my face flush. I looked for Andrew to back me up, but couldn't see him, so I continued, 'Is there any chance we can have more time to see if we can do this naturally?' My voice came out softer than I wanted.

He paused before answering.

'I'll give you two days, but understand, you need to pop then. After that, it's Easter, and you'll find me fishing down the coast.'

*

After the doctors left Andrew came and sat on the bed. He picked up the travel magazine and started reading. I slumped back in the bed. I'd already tried most natural methods to bring on labour before I was sent to hospital in the hope of avoiding being sent to hospital – raspberry leaf tea, hot curries, long walks ... but there was one more.

'Do you remember they told us in the antenatal classes that synthetic forms of oxytocin and prostaglandin are used to bring on labour?' I asked Andrew.

'Sort of,' he replied, not looking up from the magazine.

'Oxytocin is released at orgasm and there's prostaglandin in semen!'

He looked at me now with his brown eyebrows raised enough to show that some of these words were sparking interest. But I could also see his confusion, no doubt wondering why I would be talking about such things almost nine months' pregnant and confined to a hospital bed.

I took his hand. 'Let's get the real hormones, so they won't have to intervene with fake ones. Then we can still have a natural delivery and stay at the birth centre together as a family.'

'What? No way, you heard the doctor.'

I gestured for him to come closer, and whispered conspiratorially, 'Can you pick me up from Emergency? I'll call you after the three pm blood pressure check. We can go home, have sex and get back before the six pm check. We live so close.'

Andrew's butterscotch eyes lit up.

'It's our last chance,' I said.

'Last chance for sex?'

'Last chance for a natural delivery.'

I couldn't recall a chapter in *What to Expect When You're Expecting* titled, 'Escaping hospital to have sex in the hope of inducing birth naturally to avoid intervention that might lead to a caesarean', so I just had to wing it. After the three pm tests, I entered the hospital elevator and checked my appearance in the mirrors for any sign that I was an escapee. I hadn't submitted to wearing pyjamas, so I only had to cover the identity band on my wrist with my other hand.

On the ground level, I had to pass the ladies auxiliary stall where volunteers sell knitted baby booties and jumpers they make to raise funds for the hospital. These sprightly ladies watched every coming and going in the hospital and could be my undoing. Fortunately, a woman pushing a child in a wheelchair had taken their attention.

Once out of the elevator, I phoned Andrew.

'The hen has flown the coop! Meet me outside Emergency!'

*

Two days later, on all fours on the white vinyl floor of the labour ward, spotlighted in the heat and glare from a theatre light above, I had become an animal, naked and roaring. Two midwives knelt next to me. Instead of crisp white uniforms, these nurses sported goggles, shower caps, plastic aprons, gloves, green pants and green gumboots, as if they were about to clear some blockage in the sewerage system serving the Greater Sydney basin. Despite attending antenatal classes, this was not what I expected.

Six hours had passed. The pain that began as a punch across my back in the morning engulfed my lower torso by lunchtime. Then the fluid bubble my baby had bounced in for the past nine months burst onto the floor with the smell of a mouldy dishcloth. After that, it felt like bones were moving through the inside of my body, long bones, like I was birthing a giraffe. I was losing the rhythm of the long, deep breaths that had massaged the pain from the inside.

The bag with the items the midwives at the antenatal classes had advised me to bring lay abandoned in the corner. Inside it was a pretty floral cotton dress to wear while giving birth, massage oils, a hot water bottle and champagne.

I might have been better prepared if I had at least attended a birth beforehand. It was crazy to realise the only birth I'd seen was that of a family of white mice when I was in Mrs Critchlow's Year 1 class. I had carried the mouse home in a plastic cage to care for during the school holidays, not knowing she was pregnant. Without warning, hairless blobs the colour of the erasers at the end of my lead pencils tumbled out of her and fell into each other on the sawdust-covered floor of their mouse house until they again found their mother and latched on to feed. That mouse made both pregnancy and birth look effortless.

When studying psychology, I learned that much of the psychological knowledge base has resulted from experiments with mice in laboratories. As I was experiencing fundamental differences in the birthing processes to what I had observed with the mouse, so I began to see the limitations of relying on experiments with mice to understand human experiences.

Sue, one of the midwives, placed a mask over my mouth and a rush of nitrous oxide lessened the impact of each contraction. Hearing the sound of my own breath in the mask reminded me of my time scuba diving on the Barrier Reef. It gave me a rhythm as the hours passed. My eyes closed and I floated with that rhythm into an otherworld, where my focus was on the intensity of the feelings inside my body. I had disconnected with everything happening in the room except for Andrew's hands. He complained that I was squeezing them too hard, but I could not let go. His hands were my only connection with a place outside the other world of pain I'd slid into. I could hear him entertaining the midwives with jokes. He said something about me roaring like a Tyrannosaurus rex each time I moaned with pain and the mask amplified the sound. If anyone else had said that, he would have corrected them by pointing out that, 'Humans were not around when the T-Rex was around, so how could you possibly know what a T-Rex sounded like?'

My eyes were closed. I breathed with complete focus on the pain that had jammed inside me and wrapped itself around me. I began to steal nitrous oxide, sucking it in anticipation of a contraction, not just during a contraction. This did not escape Sue's notice.

'You've been labouring for hours and you look a wee bit tired. Would you like us to start the procedure for an epidural?'

I nodded. Dr Jackson was right – I didn't have thin thighs – natural delivery was not for every woman.

At that moment Andrew rallied to become my advocate.

'We don't want an epidural.'

I'd rehearsed him to say those exact words no matter how much I seemed to want pain relief. He was being an excellent advocate, doing exactly what I'd asked him to do. What he hadn't realised was that everything had changed. I'd reached a place I had no idea even existed.

'No!' My groan echoed in the plastic mask over my mouth, like a cartoon character falling off a cliff in slow motion: 'Nooooooo!'

'You heard her. No epidural. We want a natural delivery.'

'Nooooooo.'

'Too late, she's ten centimetres,' a midwife yelled from somewhere below.

Sue positioned a full-length mirror before me and I saw what looked like a rubber ball. I guessed it was a head. It occurred to me then that someone was having a baby; it took a few more seconds until I realised it was me. Then I connected back with the scene before me.

'Just a few more pushes,' the midwife said.

'A few more pushes,' Andrew repeated.

Then our baby girl arrived in an overwhelming surge.

Andrew unceremoniously cut the cord, which was twisted like a double helix. The midwives placed our daughter across my breasts. Heartbeat to heartbeat. Every colour, every sensation hummed with intensity. From this position she looked up at me and scrutinised the middle of my forehead with her dark blue newborn eyes. Looking at me as if she knew me, looking at me as if she knew much more than me.

*

Enlightenment philosopher John Locke had claimed that children were born as blank slates and everything they knew they had learned from their environment. I suspected then that John Locke had never been present at a birth.

Wrong, too, was every birth scene in Hollywood movies. In fairness, the superhuman endurance of delivery and the frisson of a new life would be difficult to reproduce in film. A photograph I saw in an art gallery once captures the endurance of delivery, without the need to show the delivery. Photographs taken just after a birth focus on the baby, but in this photo, by Rineke Dijkstra, the focus is on the mother. Titled *Julie*, the baby's face is completely hidden as Julie holds her little pink baby protectively close to her chest. Julie's large eyes show her fully alert and her hair matted. She wears only large white underpants, a pad, a wedding ring and a relaxed half smile. I think the photograph captures what it is to know how vulnerable you and your baby have been and to have both survived. And at the same time, confident that, although you have never been a mother before, you know you've got this.

Anyway, that's what I was feeling, when Dr Jackson entered the room about an hour after the birth. I wonder if he saw those qualities in me. He patted my shoulder like he had been my teammate and said, 'Well done.'

He glanced at the baby, then turned a manila folder he was carrying to show my name written along its side.

'You'll be pleased to know that I used you as a case study with the registrars to explain when not to intervene.'

I thought that without recording that intervention of a sexual nature performed outside the hospital, the validity of his study might be limited. But Dr Jackson left as quickly as he arrived, and I was in no condition to run after him to provide the details.

I returned from a shower to find Andrew on the floor at the back of the ward drinking the bottle of champagne from my bag and sucking on the hospital's nitrous oxide. Our daughter was asleep in a plastic hospital crib, wrapped as tight as a burrito in a striped bunny rug. The tiniest of Easter eggs balanced on her, lifting and lowering slightly as she slept on her side. Sue, the midwife, had placed the baby and the egg there. I had forgotten it was almost Easter.

*

I felt triumphant. We had a healthy child, we had defied the specialist's tight little circles, and our baby was no April Fool. Before leaving the hospital, I saw a mum who had been in the same pre-eclampsia group as me but she was now in a wheelchair, holding her baby. I found out from the nurses that her blood pressure had spiked during the birth to a point where it impacted her organs and tragically she suffered some brain damage. Taking matters into my own hands to avoid unnecessary intervention had thankfully worked for me and my baby, but I had been ignorant of the real risks.

We gave our daughter the name of my grandmother, Sonia, which means wisdom.

Wonder-Watching

My world shrank to the width of the house in the first two weeks after the birth. I spent this time wonder-watching. I don't remember moving from the lounge that looked like it was sewn from the von Trapp family curtains in *The Sound of Music*. I don't remember cooking or eating. I only remember the blissful feeling of Sonia's warm, peanut-shaped body lying across mine.

She looked even smaller and more protected when she was in Andrew's strong, hairy arms. Her olive skin was the same colour as his. He sang silly rhymes to her. I'd watch the brown downy hair covering her fontanel, rising and falling with each pulse, because each pulse mattered, each pulse was reassuring. I smiled at her every random suck and sigh.

We had moved for a short time into the home my grandfather had built and where Nanna and Pop lived. The gordonia, which my Nanna had planted, now reached to the height of the window, as if stretching to glimpse the newborn. It offered its first large flowers bowing to the ground, revealing its egg-yolk stamens inside circles of white, silky petals.

Bird song punctuated the day at home. Kookaburras started like old Victa lawn mowers trying to kick over during Sonia's first feed. Throughout the day rainbow lorikeets trilled in pairs around the grevillea. During the transition to golden light during her bath time, sulphur-crested cockatoos screeched a cacophonous goodnight. We had joined a raucous rhythm of life, growing and changing form.

An undisrupted night's sleep was a memory, but I took to napping like my baby. In the home, time was measured in intervals of short breastfeeds every two to three hours.

The latching on was such an unusual sensation and then I'd feel the milk rush down like an internal waterfall to my full breasts. A desert thirst immediately came to my mouth as the moisture seemed to drain directly from my body to fill my child. Her mouth moved to a suck, pause, suck, pause, suck, pause rhythm. Andrew replenished me with glasses of water.

Apparently, newborns can only see to the distance of their mother's breast. The midwife also told me that babies were already familiar with what would become their mother's breast milk. They had tasted it and smelt it because a similar substance had floated in the amniotic fluid. I believed her, because Sonia latched on tightly, as if she had been waiting nine months. From the first feed and for every feed thereafter, she gripped my index finger with her whole hand as if to ensure I wasn't going anywhere.

The first few times I breastfed, my womb contracted as if some mechanical machine were operating inside me, rotating toothed cogs against one another that tightened internal walls. When this happened, I'd sit very still and wait to see what would happen next. I had to adjust to my maternal body, as I had adjusted to my pregnant body. Vacated space inflated my belly, and milk bloated my breasts. Along with baby clothes and flowers, birthing had delivered haemorrhoids, stitches and other complications, all common after birth, but unknown to me and unexpected. Nevertheless, my body – which, before falling pregnant, I had viewed as inadequate in some way, too generous in parts, too stingy in others – now appeared to me as incredibly capable.

My body was already nourishing life when I was still lost in the marvel of creating it. I began to appreciate my body in new ways, as if it was someone else's. In fact, I was in awe of it. Previously, I'd never had a reason to think about a nipple being not just one opening, but a circle of openings. I found this out when Sonia detached herself after a feed once and milk continued to spurt at an odd angle. Not a slow drip, or a trickle, it jetted out like water from a punctured hose. During such moments, I was reminded that in Greek mythology the Milky Way was created from a spurt of Hera's breast milk. Hera was the goddess of marriage, women, the sky and the stars of heaven. I began to think perhaps it is not a coincidence that newborn babies have the same number of brain cells as there are stars in the galaxy – one hundred billion of them.

I was to discover too that even the openings of a nipple swirl in the same pattern seen in the curve of a seashell, the swirl of a fingerprint, the curl of a wave, and the eye of a storm – the same golden ratio as the DNA double helix of life itself.

Because I was reading everything about breastfeeding, I found out that even as I was wonder-watching, I was contributing to the economy. Of course I was, I was producing food that was keeping a human being alive, I just hadn't put it in economic terms. Breastfeeding is estimated to contribute $3 billion to the economy each year which is similar to the estimated contribution by the Australian movie and television production industry, however this contribution is not recognised in any economic data. Baby formula and cow's milk production is counted in gross domestic product measuring economic growth, but human milk – even if it is sold or donated – is not counted. I wondered why this was so, given the numerous benefits of breastmilk for babies. Putting wonder-watching into economic terms, the economic cost to me was about 20 hours a week of unpaid work. So early into my new role, I hoped not all my important work as a mother would be seen as unproductive by the country and having no value.

*

I displayed the cards we'd received on the mantelpiece over the fireplace, where Nanna used to place crystal vases of lilies from her garden. Sometimes when Sonia fell asleep on me, I'd remain very still, not wanting to disturb her. When Sonia finished feeding, I'd lean her over my shoulder and feel the wetness of excess milk fall from her mouth and dribble down my back. Satiated, she'd fall asleep. Her soft heartbeat pressed gently on my shoulder. I'd remain still for as long as I could. When I did move, she'd throw her arms out melodramatically, like an earthquake had struck, but settle again once I settled.

Because I was locked in one spot, I looked across to the cards for stretches of time. It was a new experience to just sit and look and feel. My favourite cards were those drawn by my nieces and nephews. They had drawn us as a family of stick figures, where we all had curly hair (even the baby) and three-digit hands. Above our curly hair they had written oversized capital letters that faced the wrong way but looked like they were aiming to spell BABY. It amused me that the other cards read, 'It's a girl!' as if the possibilities were endless, or that gender was all that mattered. I thought it odd, too, that 'congratulations' is the word to welcome a baby into the world. It isn't addressed to the newcomer. It isn't a greeting or a blessing. The congratulatory message is addressed to the parents. It's the same word trotted out for acing a test, landing a job or buying a house. I pondered why there wasn't a specific word or more precise words to acknowledge the superhuman physical and emotional effort it took to deliver life.

Some cards were addressed 'to the proud parents' and it was odd to think these were referring to us. We had gained an immediate status, as if a baby capsule in the backseat of the Toyota Corolla suddenly made us accomplished. The word 'parent', being both noun and verb, loaded us up with action and potential, but 'child', being only a noun, keeps a child passive. The English language implies our child is empty until spoon-fed with parenting. Our child, however, was not having any of that. She was already an active participant in her own development. She dictated the routines to be followed and who was to perform them. Dad was chosen for fun and laughter, Mum for cuddles and food, and her Nanna for getting her to sleep.

*

My motherhood story could end here, as motherhood stories often do, with a perfectly happy family swaddled in pastel terry towelling and smelling of breast milk. But that would be like writing a travel story while sipping cocktails in the transit lounge, having never left the airport.

Attachment

In the hospital when Sonia was born, the midwives had been quick to connect us skin to skin, knowing its importance for bonding and attachment – but this was not always the case. For my mother, giving birth in the late 1960s, her newborn was separated from her and stored in a cot in a large nursery, fed on a rigid schedule dictated not by the baby's crying, but by the matron, to fit with hospital routines. Giving birth for my mum must have been a lonely and frightening affair. She had no say in the birth process and no partner or friend present. My father was shooed away from the maternity ward – his child was not his business. This gendered demarcation sanctioned by the health system at my birth continued in our house throughout my life. My mother's work was inside the house and my father's work was outside it. Dad never saw the inside of our school, or came to watch my sister and I play netball or perform in concerts. Growing up, we all thought this was perfectly normal.

The birth classes we'd attended focused on the birth, not on preparing us to be mothers and fathers. Luckily, my mum and my friends I studied social work with, Georgette and Linda, were on hand to help us with early parenting tasks. Georgette and Linda were both the eldest children from large families, so they knew more than we did about babies. Andrew and I had never been responsible for a baby before we were presented with our own. Linda was at our house when something called the meconium poo, a newborn's bodily emission the colour of Vegemite, delivered itself on the change table like a never-ending Spanish churro winding around itself onto a plate. Linda sprang into action, scooping it up with a handful of wet wipes. Andrew and I were shocked that this mess had come from inside our tiny baby and we probably just stood looking on, horrified or giggling.

I don't think Andrew and I had thought too much about the reality of parenting before we actually were parents. I suppose parenting had been happening all around us, but parenting, like poverty, can be invisible if you choose not to notice it.

But we were not untypical first-time parents. I recall a study at the time asking parents their motivation for having a baby. Almost every couple said they thought having a baby would make them happy. Few apparently chose to have a baby in order to make the baby happy – although I'm sure that's what they meant, as did we.

Even though would-be parents expect that a baby will bring happiness, babies can be surprisingly oblivious to this expectation. By week four, Sonia, who up to then had been placid, began to *waahaahaa* and *waahaahaa* like an alarm for which we had forgotten the disarm code. She continued for hours while Andrew and I passed her back and forth between us like a ticking bomb. This only led to louder distress. I called my mum, who lived close by. She promptly arrived and placed

Sonia belly down along her upturned forearm. Sonia became as peaceful then as if she were being rocked in a hammock under a palm tree in Fiji. In the sunlight, softened by the intricate lace curtains that hung in my Nanna's house, I saw my mother as the beautiful, young, attentive mother she must have been when I was the baby crying incomprehensibly.

I'd also never thought of the deep emotional connections to the word 'mother' until I became one. 'Mother' was voted the most beautiful word in the English language in a British Council survey run in forty-six countries. 'Mother' beat words such as 'love' and 'passion'. But mother love, it seems, can be taken too far. 'Mothering' is still often used to imply fussing and overprotection. With a different intention, 'Mother' was chosen as the name for a drink laced with caffeine and sugar because it provided 'eight-cylinder energy'. And the Mother of All Bombs (MOAB) is the nickname for the world's most destructive bomb, GBU-43/B Massive Ordinance Air Blast (MOAB). MOAB was released on Afghanistan in 2017. The devastation caused by this ten-kilogram bomb did not raise as much media attention as the condemnation by Pope Francis to the use of the word 'mother' in relation to killing life, instead of the use of the word 'mother' in bringing life.

The word 'father' does not seem to carry as much emotional baggage. 'Fathering' a child can be as benign as confirming that sperm has hit its target. The connection between fathers and their children has only recently attracted the same psychological research interest as the bond between mothers and children. Studies over the last few decades show that a father's love and attention influence a child's development in different and separate ways to that of a mother's. Studies that measured fathers' interactions at an early age and their children's wellbeing years later show that children do best when they have a secure relationship with both their mother and father, especially when the relationship between the mother and father is warm and affectionate.

*

As a new mother, I knew I was falling in love with my child and my baby was responding to my love, so I was in turn falling more in love with my baby. As a social worker, I knew this as a process of bonding and attachment. I had never thought about these words before, but 'bonding' and 'attachment' were words that could merely reflect the qualities of glue and paper clips. They suddenly seemed so inadequate to reflect the magic that happens.

Social workers are sometimes called on to assess the quality of the attachment between children and their parents, because the quality of this relationship is considered so vital to the child's future development. When I came across new mothers, I was attuned to check for signs of post-natal depression. At friends' baby showers, instead of romper suits and day spa vouchers, I was the friend who gave books on post-natal depression and the phone number of support services, so they might recognise the signs early and seek help.

Since becoming a mother, it seemed strange to me that someone not experiencing my particular new and complex feelings should have already assessed them, and those of my baby. I've heard such a variety of feelings expressed by new mothers to know that each one feels something unique. Some mothers deal with the complexities of post-natal depression; some feel overwhelmed by the sense of responsibility.

The words 'bonding' and 'attachment' seemed inadequate to capture the range and depth of everyone's feelings. My professional knowledge was challenged with each new experience that didn't have a theory to support it and each new emotion that didn't have a language to describe it.

Just as when I was studying developmental psychology. My first niece was a toddler at the time and this was convenient for me to test the theories I was learning. I put her through a battery of mock tests. One was a re-enactment of the classic 'marshmallow delayed gratification test'. In this experiment, I placed a marshmallow on the table in front of her and explained that I was leaving the room. I instructed her that she could eat the marshmallow at any time, but if she waited until I returned, she could have two marshmallows. Every parent now records their child doing this on Facebook.

The children used in the original experiments were followed throughout their lives and it was found that children who delayed eating the marshmallow were more successful than the children who ate the marshmallow straight away. The children that could delay gratification received better grades at school, and were more successful in their careers and marriages. In my experiment, my niece ate the marshmallow. She later scored in the top one percent in the NSW Higher School Certificate and became a psychologist.

The type of attachment I'd planned to have with my baby was literal – I'd imagined my baby would be attached to my body at all times, the way I had seen children carried in villages in Africa and Central and South America. These babies were bound to their mother, or an older sibling, by a woven cloth, even while they worked. Although I had expected this literal attachment, the reality was that Sonia was heavy, I just wasn't strong enough to physically carry her for very long.

I like the established concept of the circle of security as a way to explain attachment visualised around a metaphorical circle. There is a parenting program about this. I just like the way the 'circle of security' sounds like a force field or something a superhero might construct. At the top of the circle is the support a child needs to move from to explore and learn. The bottom of the circle is the child's safe haven. It is the hug, or the motivational words, or the removal from a dangerous situation that a child might need. Then the child heads back out at the top of the circle, more secure because he or she received a loving response. The sense of security gained is the bond between the parent and child that allows a child to move in a bigger circle next time, so that the child feels safe to learn from new experiences. In this way, the relationship between caregivers and children is said to heavily influence a child's development, particularly in the early years when new experiences spark different areas of the brain to lay the path to build a complex network of meaning and understanding into the structure of their brain.

The children in the villages I visited had extremely large circles of security. Groups of children were everywhere and interacted freely with tourists, although I suspect that an adult was always watching nearby. I'd had more contact with children in these villages than I ever had with children in Australia.

I would have chosen to make a small, safe circle for Sonia. What I hadn't expected was that Sonia chose to create a large, fearless circle of exploration for herself. If Andrew or I were holding her and she saw a stranger, she'd open her arms in their direction for them to take her, while other babies the same age were fearful of strangers.

We had moved out of Nanna's house a few weeks after Sonia's birth and rented a ground-floor apartment in Bondi. If I recall correctly, I had visions of myself as a 'yummy mummy' running along the beach, pushing my baby in a buggy to meet up with other cool mums for coffee. I'd envisaged a year with free time to learn piano with my child and teach her Spanish and record every detail of her life.

The Surprise of not Being Stable

Two years passed – feeding, carrying, comforting, rocking, lifting, bathing, hand-holding, kissing, dressing, wiping, tickling, chasing, listening, watching, encouraging, worrying and trusting.

The plan for Andrew to be the main carer had been reversed when Andrew landed his first full-time job at a museum. So, I'd had to change my plans. I had the provision to work part time after returning from maternity leave, perhaps in a job-share situation, so I planned to do that. The new CEO who had arrived while I was on maternity leave and didn't know me, however, didn't believe in part-time managers, and the decision to allow it was at her discretion.

The CEO made my choices clear: I could work in a lesser role on a part-time basis, or work in my current role full time, or not work at all. She encouraged me to consider the latter of those choices by using guilt: 'If you've got a baby, why do you want to work anyway?'

A call to the Anti-Discrimination Board told me that despite the Anti-Discrimination law being introduced in 1984, mothers, or soon-to-be-mothers, were still the main victims of workplace discrimination. They quoted figures that left me without hope: 'One in two mothers experience discrimination in the workplace either during pregnancy, parental leave or on return to work.'

And: 'One in five mothers are made redundant, have their role restructured, dismissed, or their contract not renewed because of their pregnancy, when they requested or took parental leave, or when they returned to work.'

I had to make my decision about work just before Sonia's first birthday. I was still held in the embrace of a deep baby love and could not conceive of working full time. I left the permanent job I had worked for ten years to secure. I gave away the excellent income, sick leave, annual leave, contact with other adults and respect gained over years, and instead chose casual, part-time and consultancy work. The focus for me at the time was about earning the most money within the least time away from my child. Working in this gig economy, is also known as the 'mother track' because although the work is convenient while raising children, the lack of job security, promotions, annual leave, sick leave, long service leave and superannuation can send women backwards, financially and leave her insecure in retirement.

I noticed that because I was in casual or part-time roles that were at a lesser status than my previous management role, I was often treated as if I was new to the workforce. I had to keep my eye on the actual award rates and conditions as they were not automatically given. I took on casual teaching at university and TAFE and I worked as a self-employed consultant. Andrew worked three days in the week and on weekends, so I worked on the weekdays he didn't work. We could tag team the parenting between us without childcare costs. Childcare centres' waiting lists were long, and because we had moved, we didn't have Sonia's name on any list near to us. This work pattern rested on an untested assumption that I could both work and look after our baby, in the same room at the same time.

I undertook social research and strategic planning projects for mental health services and community services. I updated my knowledge in my field. It was exciting to see that social work and psychology had moved from a focus on problems and treatments to a focus on strengths and prevention. It is easier to build on strengths than it is to eliminate problems. Brain imaging technology was updating knowledge about how children's brains develop. When I studied social work, the accepted wisdom was that personalities resulted from some mix of both nature (genetic factors) and nurture (how one grew up). Over the years, the nature versus nurture debate had moved from nature versus nurture to nature and nurture, to nature through nurture. The debate had ended forever when it was clear that people were far more complex than even psychologists and social workers could ever have imagined. It was becoming clearer that rather than nature versus nurture, as independent of one another, it was nature and nurture interacting in myriad ways that influenced outcomes. It was not just the genes a child is born with, or the family they are born into, but also the community support a family has, and the way society is structured, that influences people's personalities, their life choices and life chances. This happened through a complex interplay of factors that proved either protective or risky for development. No science can predict the significance of each factor and the impact it will have on someone's life. The focus had shifted to giving children the best possible start in life by trying to eliminate the risk factors and enhancing the protective factors.

The study of epigenetics was starting to develop at the time to suggest that even nature wasn't fixed. A trauma in childhood can adversely impact brain development and that an impact from trauma, such as anxiety, can be passed down from one generation to another via a molecular memory in DNA to make it more active in the next generation. The good news was that even children who have had a tough start to life, if loved and offered appropriate support and opportunities, can find the resilience to bounce back.

*

On our genogram, Sonia was represented as a circle that descended from the line connecting Andrew's square and my circle. The addition of her little circle didn't go anywhere towards showing the joy she had brought to the family. Nor did it show the other changes a baby had brought: the reconfiguration of the house, the loss of sleep, the disconnection from the working world, the loss of friends who didn't have children and the decimation of a social life.

I was exhausted from running in her orbit, but I didn't hesitate when the opportunity came to do it all again. We tried for a second baby and we were relieved when our doctor again confirmed that we had defied that gynaecologist's meticulous little circles.

With my second pregnancy, I experienced a special treat that I couldn't have with the first pregnancy. I could enjoy feeling the baby inside me react to Sonia's hand on my belly and talking into my bellybutton as if it were a microphone to the baby's ear.

We sold the apartment I'd had since my single days, and placed a deposit on a house.

On the morning of the move, my parents took Sonia so that Andrew and I could pack up the house without her tripping between our legs or being hurt in the furniture-removal process. I remember I wore a light-blue cotton maternity dress because it was so humid. The antique silky oak wardrobe stood on the front lawn amongst the other furniture inherited from Andrew's grandmother. There was a chest of drawers, a music cabinet, an oval dining table and six chairs which we had transported down from her Queenslander. They looked like museum pieces and drew comments from people passing to or from the beach. It was disconcerting to have everything normally kept inside the house out on public display.

The sun reflected off the large oval mirror on the wardrobe into my eyes as I passed in and out of the house, carrying items too small for the removalist's van, breakables like vases and china, and placed them in my car. Dust from these wiped onto my dress, leaving streaks of grey on its white flowers. I felt the dust on my hands and on my sweaty face, too.

The removalists had already packed the cot, change table, the 'von Trapp family lounge' and our beds into the van, when they began to question if all the furniture would fit. The removalist in charge sat on our dining table on the lawn as he calmly suggested we hire another removalist for the rest of the furniture. It was not clear if the removalist had a genuine problem, or didn't want to do all the work. We had provided him with an itemised list, but perhaps he hadn't anticipated the size and heaviness of the antique furniture. The problem was, we had to vacate the property that day and our belongings were already on the street. We agreed that he should put the largest items in the van and after that we could assess the situation. Our chances of finding another removalist at such short notice were incredibly slim.

As I walked into the house to carry more packed boxes to the car, Andrew walked out of the house towards me empty handed. I thought he was doing this just to give me a hug or a kiss. Instead, he grabbed me in the doorway. He came in close to my face as I prepared for a kiss. But there was no kiss.

'Fix this mess,' he said with a clenched jaw and a tight mouth. He pushed me backwards in the doorway. 'Fix it!'

I felt the heat from his palms and the touch of his fingers high up my arms, but wasn't conscious of the pressure – so hard that it left marks.

'Fix it!'

I'd never experienced this before: the surprise of not being stable. For this reason, I suppose, I didn't resist being pushed. I didn't throw my arms out to try to stabilise or grab hold of something. I just tried to take in what was happening, I tried to stay standing as my centre of gravity shifted as he kept pushing me.

If the removalist saw anything, he said nothing. If the young crowds passing to and from the beach saw anything, they said nothing. Andrew said nothing. I assumed he was ashamed of his behaviour. I was in shock. I said nothing. As I walked inside the house, my heart was racing at the same time as I instinctively bandaged my hands around the small life inside me: 'It'll be alright. It'll be alright.'

*

As a social worker, I should have remembered that violence towards women by their partner often first happens when the woman is pregnant. Being pregnant, I had felt at the height of my bodily powers, creating new life and nourishing life, but the incident made it clear that I was also at my most vulnerable.

Journey of a New Planet Earth Dweller

The house we bought had been advertised as a four-bedroom colonial cottage. It was in a bush setting and was hugged by well-established trees. On our street, a forty-kilometre-per-hour symbol was painted in yellow. It reflected the real pace of this suburb that seemed forgotten by Sydney's frenetic high-rise pace. The 'village', as it was known, maintained its sleepiness like the oysters lining the spectacular bay surrounding it. At the end of our road was a school in a bush setting, and beyond that a natural parkland that extended to the river.

When we moved into our house, neighbours greeted us with gifts and offered help. It was rare in Sydney to find a genuinely close-knit community like this. We knew we'd found the ideal suburb in which to raise children.

Our garden had established trees in the backyard, and Linda, Georgette and Mum brought more trees and helped us plant them in our front garden. Inside, I found a sunny spot to place the von Trapp family lounge in anticipation of wonder-watching a new baby. In its position I could relax and look into the backyard and a eucalypt with decades of growth. It spread its branches the length of the large windows. The tree offered sanctuary for large birds that announced their landing and departure throughout the day. Its bark and kindling were used to fuel our fireplace. The jacaranda that grew close to the verandah dropped its purple flowers in November and turned the backyard into an impressionist painting.

Despite our idyllic family home, the incident on the moving day concerned me. It made me feel that my home life now involved some level of risk, and my home life was increasingly becoming my whole life. The incident made me feel like I knew my husband less and this made me feel less secure in myself and my own judgement.

Sitting on the lounge, looking at the jacaranda, I noticed for the first time just how close it was planted to the kitchen and that it leaned towards the house. I noticed, too, that the eucalypt's magnificent branches could drop without warning. I began to think about the threat posed by the surrounding bush as bushfire season began. Our home, advertised as a four-bedroom colonial cottage, was in reality a three-bedroom house with an office, clad with wood panels to hide fibro sheeting.

*

I came across Sonia's memory book as I was unpacking. It had been a present from Nicola and her husband, Rob, when Sonia was born. Popular memory books at the time featured glossy photographs of babies dressed with mermaid tails, or angel wings, or babies that were photographed inexplicably sitting inside flowerpots or snail's shells. Compared to these books, my friends had chosen an unconventional baby book, made of hard cardboard and coarse recycled paper. Titled,

Journey of a New Planet Earth Dweller, it encouraged parents to literally see their children as if from another planet, to see them as aliens, and to be fascinated with their alien behaviour. It asked parents to note their alien's time of touchdown, where they landed and who assisted with the landing. It encouraged the recording of their alien's likes and dislikes, what made them giggle, what mischief they got up to on this planet, their alien sayings and so on. I appreciated the honesty of this approach to parenting – viewing our own offspring as alien but intelligent life forms. This book encouraged parents to take on the role of observer and recorder to create the story of their child's life. Observer and recorder were natural roles for me, ones that I enjoyed.

I turned the recycled paper pages of the memory book with the reverence afforded a medieval illuminated tome. A photograph from Sonia's second birthday party featured on the most recent pages. I had chosen just one photograph and it was taken after the party, when she had removed all her clothes except for her Dorothy the Dinosaur undies. In the photo, she is sitting on an outdoor chair, eating her dinosaur birthday cake. More cake is caught in the wispy blonde hair falling around her face than is reaching her mouth. This photo shows that Sonia had enjoyed her party, but the photographs I didn't include were a reminder that the first child's birthday party we hosted as parents had not quite been a success.

In the lead-up to the party, I had painted over the green hallway that the previous owner had stencilled with homely patterns of ducks. I also painted the handrail on the stairs, which looked grubby and worn. Andrew watched *Seinfeld* repeats as I painted. I asked for his help. He responded that he saw nothing wrong with the paint that was there.

I got on with preparations for the party. Coming from a family where buying a birthday cake would be a sign of both waste and failure, I made the cake. I also made a papier-mâché piñata by covering a large balloon with glue-soaked newspaper, which had to be left to dry for days before painting it. I cooked food to cater for twenty children, one with a peanut allergy, and fifteen adults, four vegetarians and three that were gluten free. I made party bags and organised games to run to a schedule. My mother was assigned the craft table, Linda was in charge of active games and Georgette ran pass-the-parcel.

The repetition of the comment 'we didn't realise Sydney stretched this far', as each family from the Bondi playgroup arrived, made it clear that we were never going to see these families in our suburban home again. But it was the ill-judged party theme of spiders that warranted them looking at us from their car windows as if we were the Addams Family as they drove away.

In my defence, Sonia loved visiting the museum where her dad worked. When strangers asked her what sort of things she liked, hinting at princesses or dolls, Sonia answered, 'Skeletons, pharaohs and dinosaurs.' When other children might have cuddled a teddy bear for comfort at night, Sonia slept soundly with a muttaburrasaurus.

At the time of her second birthday, 'Daddy's museum' was holding a spider exhibition featuring tarantulas, iridescent dancing peacock spiders and other exotics from jungles around the globe. Sonia had visited the exhibition many times and found 'biders' fascinating. It was obvious that her birthday piñata had to be a red-back spider.

When the families arrived, Sonia greeted her guests with spider tattoos on her arms and legs. Then she led her two-year-old guests to pass under Australia's largest red-back spider to enter the backyard. It hadn't occurred to me that not all two-year-olds were as fond of spiders as my daughter until I heard their wails, and saw them run to the safety zone behind Mum's or Dad's legs.

*

Turning the pages of the memory book, I was reminded that Sonia always slept with one arm punching the air, as if she also celebrated the victory that is putting a baby to sleep. Between the pages for photographs were paper pouches for childhood mementos. Inside these were fossilised footprints and handprints at three months and six months recorded in paint on paper from a time long past. Inside, too, were soft strands of baby hair collected from her pillow, and the plastic-coated hospital identity band wrapped around her ankle soon after her birth. The circumference looked smaller than a twenty-cent coin.

When I became a mother, my own mother gave me the album from when I was a baby. It was intended to record the highlights of my early years, but it is mostly blank. The pages for photos are also blank. The fact that I was child number three might explain these omissions. It had the uninspiring title of *Baby Album*. These words were written in white over a dusty pink cover, the colour of a cashmere sweater a librarian might have worn at the time. My brother's baby album cover was blue, the colour of a clear sky on a promising spring day. Inside the covers, both books are the same. There are two pages to record the baby's weight with a chart to plot the age in weeks on the X-axis and the weight on the Y-axis. My mother completed this chart and a dental diagram showing the order in which my teeth arrived. It looks as though the global food corporation Nestlé produced *Baby Album*. Below the dental chart and the weight chart are images of Nestlé Chicken Broth and Nestlé Chicken Dinner. Breastfeeding is not mentioned in this book, possibly because Nestlé make formula. On one page, a chart titled 'Educational diet' instructs novice parents to introduce strained fruit at two months and junior foods at seven months. This differed from the advice the early childhood nurse gave to me.

The closest reference to a child's personality, emotions or behaviour appears on the page titled, 'Baby's Habits'. A full-page column leaves space for parents to list baby's 'Good habits' down one side. I laughed when I saw that the column next to it was headed, 'Baby's bad habits and when they disappeared'.

This book tells me a lot, not about me as a baby, because this section is also empty, but about the society I entered into. It presented what appears as an organised world, where parents had a clear role in controlling a childhood that ran to a strict routine, with more than a nod to Nestlé's commercial interests in the real-life era of *Mad Men*. Children were not aliens; they were not unknown persons with unique likes and dislikes. Children were predictable; they doubled their birth weight in six months and grew teeth in a set pattern. Baby care was rational and measured. Good behaviours were noted and bad behaviours quickly 'disappeared', with no need to explain how this might be achieved. Children's personalities were not relevant. This book made it clear that mothers were naturally capable of doing all that was required of them.

*

The other book my parents started when I was born was a bank book. It was also the colour of a librarian's cashmere sweater and my brother's was also the blue of the sky on a clear spring day. As well as offering a glimpse into life before internet banking, these two books offer a glimpse into parenting goals from that era:

1. To keep your children physically healthy.
2. To provide for your children financially.

The first responsibility was my mother's and the second was my father's.

Sonia's 'Blue Book', the official child's *Personal Health Record* created by the NSW Department of Health and given to all mothers in hospital soon after the birth of their baby, probably evolved from the baby album my mother was given when she gave birth to me. In the Blue Book I was given the commercial interests of baby food companies had disappeared when I received Sonia's, but the emphasis on physical health remained. There was almost no focus on the child's social or emotional development. This baby manual lacked the simple operating instruction, 'Show your child they are loved'.

The Blue Book also lacked a place where I could record or reflect on Sonia's inquisitiveness. She conducted experiments to discover how many fingers she could fit in her mouth at once, and she gathered words with the exuberance of a tourist. There was nowhere in the book to record special moments or the conversations she held with herself in the language of her own making.

The book was to be taken to early childhood appointments where the nurse would record baby weights and measures and plot child growth. The focus on plotting growth made parenting look more like we were growing bean sprouts than parenting a human. On our first visit to the child health nurse, she weighed and calculated our baby from every angle.

Andrew and I had nervously laid our naked baby on her lambskin rug like a sacrifice in preparation for the examination. So much of the consultation time was taken up by the repeated pulling and pressing and popping and testing for clicky hips that it seemed to me a sure way for a baby to develop some.

As her daily companion, Sonia forced me to notice details and sensations I hadn't noticed, or had stopped noticing. My pace slowed to that of her early tentative steps as she tried to understand the fascinating world around her. She'd pick out individual stones in the footpath or reach to grab an ocean wave. In exchange for Sonia's teachings, I wanted to draw her attention to the perfection in an egg, the precision of a spider's web, the mystery of silkworms, the personalities of dogs, and so much more.

Being made to stop and learn through a child's eyes was an unexpected joy, one that I didn't think parenting classes or advice books made enough of. While I approached parenting as a heart and head affair, parenting information seemed to focus on the work of the hands. Classes reduced parenting to tasks – feeding, sleeping, limit-setting. They didn't promote the love and fun that children can bring, or the philosophical aspects of being a mother that were fascinating to me. Perhaps I'm unusual in this. I once happened to say, 'It's as if I'd never felt love before I had my baby', or words to that effect, to another mother when we were both confined in the 'mother's room' feeding and changing nappies at the local Westfields shopping centre. As she finished sticking the tabs to her baby's nappy, she looked at me as if I was a freak, before she left with the parting words, 'I just get on with it.'

Olivia

By June I became one of those mothers every other mother hates – the one who says, 'Giving birth didn't hurt a bit!' This is because, thankfully, my second baby slipped effortlessly into the world. Unrelenting vomiting with each contraction apparently helped to push the baby along and speed the process, even though this technique hadn't been discussed in birth classes.

While driving to the hospital, Andrew had had to pull over to the curb not far from home so I could throw up in the gutter. As we drove off, I saw that we had been positioned under the council sign that welcomes visitors to the suburb. It boasts of the suburb's award-winning status as a 'Tidy Town'. Before that, I'd spent the morning on my bed vomiting into suitable receptacles, with Sonia curled in next to me. My mum, Georgette and Andrew had also been coming and going from the bed. Mum held a damp face washer on my forehead, just as she had done whenever I was sick as a child and this brought me great comfort. Declining the opportunity to be part of the birthing process, Mum took Sonia to look after her at her house. Andrew drove Georgette and I to the hospital.

I'd invited Georgette to be part of the birth process this time. I wanted to offer her the opportunity to attend the birth of the child who would become her godchild and I also wanted her to be with me. Not long after university, Georgette had been told she had one year to live. She had been diagnosed with a rare cancer. But she was strong and determined. She had already been living for eight years more than the experts had given her. She was in a relationship, she managed her own health and she lived and worked on her own terms, with some modifications and limitations. What surprised her was that when she visited her oncologist, not once did he say: 'Sorry we got it wrong', or, 'Let's learn more about you and what you are doing to find out why you are so healthy'.

As we passed the theatre where I had previously delivered, the smell of hospital antiseptic brought back memories of my birth experience with Sonia. This was muddled by the scent of patchouli fired in oil burners as we approached the birth centre. Andrew and Georgette propped me on a chair at the entrance. I looked across to a poster on the opposite wall. On it was the silhouette of a mother lifting her child in the air. It read, 'To the world you might be just one person, but to one person you might just be the world.' Since becoming a mother, I had noticed that cheesy inspirational statements now held gravitas for me. The poster steeled me to make my way inside and do whatever would be required.

The birthing room was cosy and featured a four-poster double bed with a floral bed cover, pine bedside tables, speakers and a television. Georgette chose the type of relaxing music played by massage therapists that featured the Australian birds I'd heard in my garden that morning. Then Deb the midwife arrived. She asked for permission to examine me.

'Ten centimetres.'

'Already?'

I was comfortable enough, chatting and vomiting, then I said with an urgent tone, 'I think the baby's coming!' Moments later, without a sign of struggle, our gorgeous baby arrived. The lack of struggle left me a bit blasé, until I saw in Georgette's face the astonishment of seeing a birth for the first time. Almost immediately, the midwife had prepared a tepid spa and she ushered us into it. I floated skin to skin with this warm, wondrous being, known, but unknown to me. I felt the same intense love at the sight of our baby, as I had done when Sonia was born. We called her Olivia because she had come into the world so peacefully. The olive branch being a symbol of peace, and Olivia was an old-fashioned name, which seemed fitting for our wrinkly winter baby soon warmed by a woollen cardigan knitted by her grandmother.

A fresh circle could be added to our genogram, filling in more white space around us. A family of four – there was a solid Henry Moore sculptural quality to that.

*

My body still held the warmth of the spa as our visitors brought a little of the cold winter's day inside with them. Sonia, having been told to be extra gentle, air-kissed her sister on the forehead, then tried to hold her doll-like hand, which she couldn't prise open. Despite my objections to gender-stereotyped toys, Sonia always chose the pink aisle at toy shops, so perhaps it was no surprise that Mum and Dad bought Sonia a Ballerina Barbie as a gift to keep her from being jealous of her new sister. Sonia updated each of the nursing staff as they entered the room: 'I got baby sista!' and, 'I got Ballerina Barbie!'

My dad fled the room at the slightest sign that I was about to breastfeed. As I fed Olivia, Sonia 'breastfed' her Ballerina Barbie through her belly-button on the bed next to me. Later, when I changed Olivia's nappy, Sonia made me pretend to change her nappy too, even though she'd been wearing underpants for months.

When Dad returned, I placed his youngest grandchild in his oversized, calloused hands. These were hands that had been scrubbed to remove the grease from the creases each night with Solvol (a cake of soap that looked and felt like it was made of metal filings). His arms had rarely held a baby. He was awestruck. But, while he was holding Olivia, I saw vulnerability in my father for the first time. My dad wore a puffy jacket, which he didn't take off, but even with his jacket on, I could tell he'd lost weight. He had suffered a heart attack not long after Sonia was born and he had not returned to his old self. In fact, he had softened.

When I was five, I'd won a painting competition for a portrait of my father. I don't know why, but I'd painted him in a suit and a bowler hat. He was holding an umbrella in the rain, waiting for a bus to take him to work. Not being that experienced at painting, I had dipped the brush in the water too often and the water had dripped down the paper as I painted. This unintended effect increased the realism of the rain. The life-sized raindrops that fell on my father at the bus stop must have bumped me up a notch against the other five-year-olds in the competition. The father I painted resembled the fictional father in *Mary Poppins* more than it resembled my actual father. The painting might have expressed exactly what the organisers of the Father's Day competition wanted: that is, no matter what the weather, a father does whatever is required to look after his family. My father did look after his family no matter the weather, but he did it in a very different way to the father I had painted. As a mechanic, Dad wore overalls, not a bowler hat or a suit. I remember the company's uniform when I was that age; they wore electric-blue overalls with two orange stripes down the side. He looked to me like the coolest racing car driver. He never caught a bus – he drove – and he would have considered carrying an umbrella unmanly. But as he was standing there, with Olivia in his arms, I saw my father's eyes well up and I also saw him pretend it was from laughter.

'She's got wingnuts for ears,' he said and handed Olivia back to me, as if she was faulty. I was used to digs like this, the type of humour that was only fun if you weren't on the receiving end of it. Ordinarily, a poke like this would send me into a defensive mode, but my perfect newborn did not have wingnut ears; she just needed more hair. On the other hand, Dad had wingnut ears, so he might have been claiming my child as one of his tribe. Besides, I imagine a mechanic might value wingnuts.

*

It was quiet again when my parents left the birth centre with Sonia. Deb and Georgette started to fill a plastic hospital cot with water to make a shallow bath. Olivia cried for the first time, as she was undressed. Georgette formed a boat with her elegant hands, floating Olivia's body back and forth slowly through the water. I tried to find the words to describe the intense love I felt for my daughter. Georgette knew there are more words in Arabic to describe feelings of love, than there are in English, but she didn't know Arabic well enough to say if they were words exclusive to the love a parent felt for a child, which English lacked. The word soulmate, not usually applied to babies, the concept of feeling a deep natural affinity was the closest to how I felt.

We talked about how at school and university we had studied English literature that focused on romantic love, but we never read literature where a mother or father wrote about the depth of love for their child. At University we read the romantic poets, Plutarch, with his endless metaphors for love, and Donne and Marlowe's clever conceits of sex, which they used to lure women to their bedchambers. As schoolgirls we had been struck by the violent passion of Heathcliff and Catherine, and obsessed with the genteel respect of Darcy and Elizabeth, but I don't recall literature exploring a parent's love for a child.

It was David Lodge who wrote, in *The British Museum is Falling Down*: 'Literature is mostly about having sex and not much about having children. Life is the other way around.'

The voices of mothers in English literature in particular seemed to be missing, they were written about, but they were not the ones doing the writing.

Long before studying literature, the children's stories I read also set me up with ideals of romantic love. In fairytales, and in Disney films, princesses fall in love with princes who rescue them from life as a mermaid or one hundred years of sleep. Oddly, these stories for children were not about loving parents, quite the opposite, in fairytales, parents, or specifically stepparents, used their children and stepchildren as domestic slaves to clean fireplaces, or they left them stranded in the forest.

*

After the bath, Georgette laid a pink-skinned Olivia on a fresh towel and parcelled her arms and legs into a terry towelling jumpsuit. I watched Georgette pin a brooch to the jumpsuit. The brooch looked like a series of circles that resembled an eye. A cool Mediterranean-blue pool with a white centre dotted with black. It was encased in a delicate circle of gold. She had ordered it from Lebanon in preparation for her new godchild. I'd seen this symbol often travelling in Turkey, Greece and the few countries I'd been to in the Middle East. It was a talisman for protection. I thought of this as a different circle of security for Olivia. If someone commented on Olivia's beauty or cuteness, Georgette would immediately counteract any jealous curse by a set response in Arabic that protected against it. Since Olivia's birth, Georgette had to say these words many times, and Olivia behaved as if she felt secure in that protection.

Until my new practical role as a mother, I couldn't seem to find common ground between my beliefs and the beliefs my family held. The role of mother was one my family could relate to and approve of. Being a mother also made me appreciate the sacrifices, hard work and the love they had afforded me and I realised they had been given very little thanks for it, so I tried to address this.

Since I had last given birth, I had read that science would explain my intense love for my newborn as a chemical reaction from hormones released during pregnancy and birth. Like a love potion, endorphins had helped me to endure labour, and oxytocin and dopamine helped us both to bond. I found it fascinating that a father's testosterone levels can plummet after the birth and that extra oestrogen can be made so that he can become more sensitive to oxytocin and dopamine, so he, too, can fall in love with his newborn. Being in the birth centre offered Andrew and Olivia this opportunity that was never offered to my father and me. It was fascinating to read that adoptive parents and adoptive children, too, can get the same rushes of dopamine when they spend time together. In fact, I once read a study that found a person who loses their wallet is more likely to have it returned if they have a photograph of a baby inside, because the sight of the baby causes the finder to release oxytocin, making them feel more loving and kinder.

Scientific explanations of our new attachments don't leave much scope for spiritual ones. One of my friends believes that children choose their parents based on what they have to learn in their current spiritual life. If this were true that would make parents not just a child's first teacher of behaviour and early literacy; children, too, would be their parents' teachers and partners in this expansive spiritual mission. I'd prefer to think of my children, Andrew and I as partners in something large and meaningful, rather than to think we were simply responding to chemicals in our bodies in a predetermined way. Perhaps one does not have to exclude the other.

*

When Georgette left, Andrew, who had rocked Olivia back to sleep after her bath, gently placed her back in the plastic hospital cot, which Deb had magically converted back from a bath to a bed. I waited for Andrew to join me, lying on the bed. Instead, he sat on the edge of it and used the remote to switch on the television. I had forgotten what day it was, but the football was on. I looked across to Olivia, worried the television noise would wake her, but it didn't. Sitting behind Andrew, I noticed his brown hair roots growing out of the blond, revealing a thin gash of brown down the centre of his head. I looked across to the exquisite miniature tulips sent to us by his sister in Brisbane and noticed intricate patterns of darkness at the base of each petal. The bedspread and curtains that I thought had given the room a homely feel on our arrival now looked dated with the ambience of a roadside motel.

'What an amazing day!' I patted the bed next to me. 'Come and lie down,'

Andrew picked up the remote to switch off the TV and joined me on the bed. I spooned into his back, briefly feeling his body press into mine with each breath. My hands softly explored his chest hairs. Before long, he was snoring. After a few rounds of this snoring, I peeled myself away stealthily, so as not to wake him, and pulled my body up onto the bed. I turned and lifted Olivia, enfolding her into the warmth of the bed. I almost wanted her to wake so I could see her eyes and we could interact, but she remained blissfully ignorant of my desire. I built a love fortress with my body around her and watched her chest rising and falling under the pastel blanket. Her breath kept a half-paced rhythm with her father's snores. Stroking her tufting hair with two fingers, I whispered, 'That's your daddy, Olivia. He loves you, but he's sleepy right now.'

Fight or Flight

In the early morning darkness, I arrived at the hospital where Olivia had been born only three months earlier. I wore pyjamas with a coat hastily pulled over them. As we left the car, Olivia began crying like a lamb bleating. I'd sloppily wrapped her in all the bunny rugs we had. I'd parked in the emergency bay and was running with Olivia in my arms, although I knew the emergency had passed. Mum had already told me the news on the phone. She called me last out of my siblings. She doubted whether it was right to call at all – because I had a baby.

The Emergency waiting room was fluorescent lit, but eerily quiet. It had the vibe of a suburban 7-Eleven at five minutes to 11. Without words, I was directed to a small, dim room. I opened the door and was greeted by a middle-aged social worker who introduced himself as Ben. I wanted Ben to leave. My mother, brother and sister were collected at the end of the bed and silent. I stood with them and faced my father's body lying in front of us. My father's tea-coloured skin had paled. All expression was gone. It was then I noticed tubes attached to his nose, and I wanted to pull them out. I wanted to pound on his chest. I wanted everyone to leave. I wanted this time alone with my Dad. Dad and I still had things to discuss, which I didn't want others to hear. I wanted to scream into the silence of the room.

Only Olivia wailed. I wanted to sit and talk with my dead father but I had to feed my baby daughter, and I didn't want to do both at the same time but I didn't know which to do first.

*

After I'd returned home from the hospital, Andrew found me in the kitchen, squatting on our cold wooden floorboards, tiled over with papers. I was attacking decades of paper memories with the tenacity of a swamp mosquito. I was looking for something, any sheet of paper with a trace of my father on it. Papers tiled the floor. There were cards and letters I'd kept that Mum and Dad had sent to me when I lived overseas, but Dad hadn't written on any of them. I found yellowing *Happy Birthday Daughter* cards featuring puppies or horses. These cards opened to reveal the handwritten words, 'Love, Mum and Dad.' But it was only Mum who wrote them. My dad, it turns out, had never written a word to me and I'd never noticed.

I dragged the wooden chair from the kitchen table to reach a plastic storage box from above the kitchen cupboard. These were the only papers left to look through – tax receipts. It was Dad who nagged me to keep receipts, the way Mum nagged me to always carry a cardigan. The only written trace I found of my father appeared in three columns on a loan ledger. He'd returned it to me after I'd made the final repayment on the money he and Mum had lent me for the deposit to buy my apartment, years before I met Andrew. He had drawn three columns on lined paper – DATE, AMOUNT, TOTAL. His handwriting looked like the scrawly etchings insects leave on scribbly-gum bark trees.

I could hear Andrew's Ugg boots scraping the floor behind me like sandpaper. I turned to see he was wearing track pants and a woollen jumper and rubbing his eyes. I didn't get up. He stepped over the cards and paper. He wrapped around me from behind, lifted me from the floor, and turned me around for a bear hug.

*

When we were kids, a road trip was all it took to transform Dad from a grumpy authoritarian to a happy philanthropist who bought heart-shaped ice creams for us at petrol stops along country roads. A typical Sunday involved a drive to Warragamba Dam or a display home village in what was then Sydney's outskirts. These homes were excessive by my parents' standards, some with carpets halfway up their walls, but they were exciting to us. We'd run through the houses, shouting to Mum and Dad about which ones we wanted them to buy. It took many visits before I realised we were never going to live in one. We drove to Warragamba Dam many times too, but I don't remember ever seeing it. We picnicked inside the car, enjoying cold sausages and a family block of Cadbury's Dairy Milk chocolate. After the sausages and before the chocolate, Mum would impress us by peeling the skin off green apples with a knife to form one long snakeskin that fell into the bowl on her lap. Then she'd cut the apples into pieces we had to eat before we had any chocolate. After we ate, we drove home. The snakeskin peel, holding most of the apple's nutrition intact, was disposed of in the compost.

The best road trip had been to Dad's hometown of Gilgandra. In Gilgandra, Dad had a history, a status and a confidence he didn't have living in Punchbowl. His older brother, who died flying a plane in World War II, is memorialised in St Ambrose Cathedral, where an everlasting flame dances above a brass lamp engraved with his name. I had seen this respectful memorial on the road trip with Dad. I planned to repeat this road trip to Gilgandra with my daughters. In contrast to the brass lamp memorialising his brother, for Dad I wanted to plant a tree. I chose to wait a few months, until Olivia was comfortable with eating solid food.

I thought Andrew would join us on this trip as a family, in honour of my dad. It was Andrew who Dad invited into his garage regularly for a beer before dinner, never me. I could only enter Dad's shed to inform him that dinner was ready.

*

When I first informed Andrew of the road trip he said, 'I don't understand why you're still upset about your dad dying.'

I recall we were in bed when he said this, because I remember staring at my pillow for some time afterwards. I wasn't wondering why I was still grieving; I was wondering why my husband couldn't understand why I was still grieving.

A few weeks after this conversation, when the children were asleep, Andrew and I were watching the film, *The Piano*, on television. We'd seen it before, so I knew to leave the room in anticipation of the scene where Sam Neill chops off Holly Hunter's finger with an axe. I stood to leave. Next thing I knew, I was thrown across the room as if weightless. My head hit the brick wall without a sound. I remember thinking there should have been a thwack or a bang, but there was no sound. The children didn't wake. No one came running. No siren approached. Andrew said nothing. My head thudded from deep inside. In the confusion of that moment, I had the clarity to know that everything had changed. It wouldn't matter if he never did that again; he had shown me what could happen at any random moment.

*

As a social worker, I knew about the Cycle of Violence. I'd informed other women about it and I'd taught it to welfare studies students when I was teaching at TAFE. I'd first heard the term in the late 1980s, when domestic violence was being excavated from under the thick-pile carpets of suburban homes to be recognised as a significant social issue. In my first social work role I attended training run by a community legal centre where they showed a movie titled, *Guns and Roses* – a movie that explained the Cycle of Violence. Tension, explosion, honeymoon. On one curve of the cycle there was a build-up of tension, hence the guns; the tension dissipated on the other side of the cycle, leading to remorse, hence the roses. Actors portrayed characters in vignettes that illustrated this theory. The men in those vignettes, I seem to recall, were large men with tattoos and missing teeth, so they should have been easy to spot and avoid marrying.

I never saw a Cycle of Violence in my own lounge room. We were not arguing; we were watching television. No build-up of tension. No remorse. No roses. I knew the advice: 'If it ever happens – get out!'

Fight or flight was presented as the only way humans respond to a stressful event when I studied social work. They fight or run. This was a universal scientific fact. It is on this basis that people say to women who are attacked or abused, 'Why didn't you run?', 'Why didn't you fight back?', 'Why didn't you leave?' They tend not to ask of the man abusing or attacking, 'How could you do that?' 'Why did you do that?' 'Why didn't you leave?'

This understanding of fight or flight originally came from observations of animals and then observations of male behaviour only. It is now understood that although all bodies will react to the danger in a way that will help them to deal with it, it is not a universal truth that these reactions automatically lead to fight or flight. As well as 'fight or flight', which males might favour, females often use communication skills, to reason with their attacker and seek out social support. This could be a better survival skill rather than try to attack back or flee, given their attacker will usually be stronger. In domestic violence situations this danger occurs in their own home with someone they love and trust, it is not a stranger on the street.

It is suggested that instead of releasing noradrenaline to get the blood pumping, as men do for fight or flight, women secrete endorphins to help stimulate social interactions, which also alleviates pain. This knowledge developed from experiments that have shown that when two male rhesus monkeys that are strangers are placed in a small cage together, they will fight, but two female rhesus monkeys in the same situation reduce the tension by grooming each other. Of course, no one wants to live with violence, but quite apart from experiments on monkeys, where is one to go and how is one to leave with a baby and a toddler, casual teaching jobs for income and a mortgage? And why should one have to leave their home which in fact they had paid for?

'That never happened,' Andrew said when I tried to discuss it. It was hard for me to believe it had happened, because I had never thought of him as capable of such a thing. I loved and trusted him, he was my husband and we had a binding promise to love and support each other no matter what. It was easy for him to make me think it hadn't happened, but then I would remember trying to cover up the bruised eye. It was better when the bruise turned purple, because then it looked like I was only being overzealous with my make-up and I could match it on the other side. A fellow lecturer was perceptive and asked about the eye. I hit a new low then by lying to protect my husband. I didn't feel I could tell anyone and I didn't want to lie, so I withdrew even more from friends and family.

I found myself one day just staring at the back of the classroom when I was teaching the theory of the Cycle of Violence to a class of students. I remember one of the student's faces when my attention returned to the class, the way she looked at me. I knew she knew. I stopped teaching after that.

Memorial for the Common Man

'*Toot, toot, chugga chugga big red car...*' had played too many times, but I knew not to change it. In the rear-view mirror I saw Sonia dancing as much as her car seat would allow and a disgruntled Olivia dribbling and pulling her ears. She was teething. There was a map over my thighs and the smell of eucalyptus from the small sapling on the floor in front of the empty passenger seat next to me. Secret tears slid down my face. For Olivia's sake, I had tried to stay smiling since Dad's death and the 'incident' I had with the wall. I knew that babies imitate the facial expressions of those caring for them.

'Is this where we're going to see Poppy in the jungle?' Sonia asked for the third time since we left Sydney.

'No, Sonia, we can't see Poppy, and it's the bush, not the jungle. We're going to the bush to plant this tree as a way to remember Poppy. One day you can come back here and this little tree will be as big as Poppy was.'

The occasional kangaroo in rigor mortis at the side of the road was the only image that broke the dry monotony of the bush. Crows gathered around the dead kangaroo in anticipation of the feast to come when the sun would finally pop the carcass for them, like a piñata full of candy. I also felt a strange anticipation as I drove the last kilometres of rusty track on the far side of the forested ridges and deep spires of the Warrumbungle Mountains.

The relationship between my father and I had, at times, been as harsh and unforgiving as the landscape surrounding us. Dad's first heart attack, two years before the fatal one, had transformed him. He slowed. He started to play with his grandchildren down on the floor in a way he never had with us when we were children, at their level. He showed the older grandchildren card tricks and loved telling jokes. It was as if something had been constricting his heart, leaving him in pain all his life, and the heart attack had actually released it. Good humour and stories from his childhood flowed then. Dad laughed when he told these stories, and when Dad laughed, his eyes watered at the edges. He laughed so little in life and cried even less that when he did this laughing-crying thing, I laughed and cried with him. It could have felt natural to embrace after moments like that, but we never did.

*

After six hours of driving, we passed the rusty windmills and wheat silos that signalled the entrance to Gilgandra. *Population 2900*. The buildings displayed dated marks from previous floods, reminding me of Dad's stories. As a child visiting Gilgandra, the flood marks on the buildings had seemed so unusual to me that I had half expected to see them on the calves of the people who lived there, too.

I called Andrew to let him know we'd arrived safely. I appreciated that he'd encouraged me to take the road trip and that he'd encouraged me to take Sonia and Olivia. He didn't answer, so I left a message.

In the town's library, I found a toilet with a change table. I balanced Olivia on my hip as I wrestled with a fickle folddown plastic change table. Olivia's nappy smelt like rotting mangoes and inside it was sprayed like a Rorschach inkblot test. My back was to Sonia, who was playing with her Ballerina Barbie, when she yelled out.

'Mummy, Mummy, Ballerina Barbie fell in!'

'What's that?'

'Ballerina Barbie is in there. Get her, Mummy.'

I turned. She pointed to the bin filled with dirty nappies and paper towels people had dried their hands on and other miscellaneous items.

'Oh, Sonia, I can't get her out of there.'

Olivia was kicking her chubby legs between nappy changes.

Sonia was hitting my back: 'Mummy! Mummy!'

'I'm sorry, I can't get her?' I put a fresh nappy on Olivia with some resistance from the change table.

'No! I have to show Poppy! Poppy gave me Barbie!'

'Oh darling, but Poppy?'

'Get Barbie! Get Barbie!'

Sonia screamed. Olivia cried. I was trying to bend Olivia's stiff and resistant legs back inside the jumpsuit. Olivia's crying increased the volume of Sonia's screaming and then she cried, too. With Olivia on my hip, I opened the lid to the bin. Ballerina Barbie had not fallen far, having gracefully landed in an arabesque on some soft paper towels. I hesitated, but Sonia's tears and protruding bottom lip were hard to fight. I placed my hand into the receptacle and extracted Ballerina Barbie by her hair between the tips of my thumb and index finger.

I placed the dirty nappy into the bin with the other hand by pulling my hip to one side, to cradle Olivia in tight. I then escorted Barbie by her hair to the sink and scalded her body and tutu under the hot water tap with one hand, while holding Olivia on my hip bent away from the tap with the other. I then wiped Barbie with a baby wipe and then some hand sanitiser, dried her under the hand dryer and handed her back to Sonia.

I drove through town and parked in the shade of a large eucalypt by the river. There was no one in sight. The afternoon light between the trees was beginning to soften and there was a light breeze. The car faced the Jack Renshaw Bridge that spans the Castlereagh River. Dad had often spoken of this river, dry for most of the year when the river runs below the sand. I had thought he was telling fibs. A subterranean river sounded mythical to me, and it was a fitting location to memorialise a man who kept his emotions just below the surface.

The river was not dry that day, it was a torrent, flowing so fast it collected logs and branches from the trees along its bank and moved them along with it. A blanket of light pink covered the ground, so it looked as if the sunset were upside down. Stringybarks and ancient river red gums curtained the scene.

Olivia had fallen asleep, so I called Andrew, hoping to talk, but there was no answer. I left another message.

I'd supplied Sonia with a new packet of felt-tipped markers and a colouring book to keep her occupied. I left Olivia asleep in her car seat next to Sonia not far from the river. I left the doors open for the cross breeze and I could hear if they needed me. I carried the sapling towards the river like a pallbearer. As I moved closer, I saw what I had thought was a pink blanket over the ground was knitted from hundreds of pink galahs eating seeds. Behind me, I heard a loud crack. A large branch had hit the boot of the car. My heart was pounding as I dropped the sapling and ran back to the car. Relieved, Sonia and Olivia were fine. I lifted the large branch off the boot it had lightly dented and I threw it awkwardly – "AAAAAH!" – making the galahs fly off, bickering at me in shrill tones. I stumbled backwards and the twiggy ground caught me as I landed heavily on my bum. I looked up and saw branches; below me, twigs and leaves. All around me, wherever I looked, were trees. The bush was full of trees! What a stupid city notion I had to plant a tree as a memorial for my dad in the bush.

This epiphany held me to the ground for some time. I could hear Sonia and Olivia giggling in the car behind me. I stood up to see Olivia kicking her legs vigorously, sucking her two favourite fingers. Sonia's heart-shaped face was next to her, holding a blue felt-tipped marker, but something had changed. Sonia had made a road map of Olivia's face. She'd drawn smooth, green mountains over her sister's nose and rivers in blue around her lips. Rather than looking guilty, Sonia smiled in expectation of praise for her artwork. In fact, both the topographer and the map looked pleased. I tried a stern look of disapproval, but my lips began to curl at the edges. The map drawn on Olivia's face was framed on either side by wingnut ears. I squatted down and traced the lines over her face and she giggled with delight. Both girls were bathed in the glow of the late afternoon sun, the same quality of light that had featured in my dreams recently – yellow and warm. In those dreams Dad said the words he would have written on my birthday cards and I said what I wanted to say when he was laughing and crying from his stories. A lifetime of withheld sentiments would drip from our mouths like small talk, as we passed each other on a surreal shopping centre escalator that has no end.

I wrangled Olivia out of the car seat and placed her on my hip as Sonia and I held hands and strolled along the riverbank. I called Andrew. He didn't answer. It was after five o'clock. We walked further. I looked at my phone. I sat down on the twiggy grass again, this time with Olivia in my lap, and rang again. Olivia began a mantra that didn't end, '*Dadadadadadadad*'. Sonia, sitting next to us, placed her hand on Olivia's arm, moved in close to her face, and said, 'It's okay, Daddy's at work with dinosaurs and biders.' I was no longer convinced of this. My stomach was a knot. Instead of staying in Gilgandra that night as planned, I began the drive home. Olivia cried as I drove out of town, but it wasn't long before the movement of the car soothed her into openmouthed cherub inertia, next to her sister holding Ballerina Barbie. I caught a glimpse of the sapling, back on the floor in front of the passenger seat, each time I looked at the phone, waiting for it to light up.

Seven pm. Mudgee. Organic baby food from a jar. Nappy change. Hot chips. Coffee.

Seven-thirty pm. I called his mobile. Questioned if I should call the police.

Olivia in her pram. Walked up Church Street. Walked down Church Street. Called again. Sonia heard the panic in my voice. I stopped leaving messages. Barrelled pram into boot. Strapped children in. Explained we were driving home. Olivia cried herself to sleep.

High beams on. High beams off. Lurching into highway darkness propelled by questions that fanned raging terrors.

Eleven pm. Home. Newspaper on lawn still wrapped in plastic. Girls asleep. Carried to bed. I lay next to Sonia, more for my sake than hers, and felt bad for doing so. I wished on the fluorescent stars stuck to her ceiling. Olivia snored.

I rang again. Still no answer. I paced. I rang again.

Midnight. He answered.

'I've been so worried,' I told him.

'Sorry, I didn't see your calls. I was busy at work, then we all went out for drinks. Did you plant the tree? How's Sonia, how's Olivia?'

'Andrew, where are you?'

'Home, of course. Where else would I be?'

'Andrew, where are you?'

'Don't you believe me?'

'No.'

Silence.

'You're such a psycho bitch!'

DUCT TAPE

Why?

I paced in the kitchen, back and forth, back and forth, in front of the fridge. Stomping and sighing and growling and cursing. I chewed on the thick wick of skin surrounding my thumbnail. Olivia was asleep. Sonia was playing in the backyard under the jacaranda. I watched her from the kitchen window as she ran back and forth through the sprinkler. Water droplets made crystal in exposed sunshine fell in patterns around her. It was hard to imagine a happier child or a more joyful image of childhood.

On the fridge, Sonia's magnetic, upper-case letters were left in disarray as if shouting at me that words were not going to help, no matter how colourful. I wanted to slough off the magnets with a dramatic windscreen-wiper movement of my forearms, but I had to stay calm and wait for the neighbour to take the children to her house before Andrew and I could talk.

*

As I opened the door to our room, he was sitting on the bed with his shoulders slumped. His head hanging, his neck exposed. He looked like someone gathering his story before entering court. I remained standing, my head throbbing with questions, but only one screamed out of me – at a high pitch.

'Why?'

My arms spoke in gestures large and demanding.

'Why?'

I got answers to the where and what and how and who, but the why was elusive. It made my hunger for it more insatiable. His answers prompted a new question.

'How could you?'

This was a rhetorical question, but, contrite, he answered: 'It didn't start as anything, we just went to the movies.'

'The movies? Why didn't you take me to the movies?'

'You were busy with the kids.'

That's how it arrived, blunt and honest: 'You were busy with the kids.'

He didn't try to recover those words or package them differently. I saw that it was only after their release that these words gave him the understanding that I, too, now had.

'Leave!' I screamed in a tone I'd never heard from myself before. It was a tone that made the neighbourhood dogs bark. I walked briskly behind him to the front lawn, escorting him off the premises. As he approached the front gate, I picked up the dew-filled newspaper roll from the lawn. I threw it at his back and a spray of water flew into the air. It fell slightly short of him, but I wished it hadn't.

*

Perhaps those lines drawn on the genogram were only drawn in pencil and so could be easily erased. Perhaps a thin line was all that was holding us together. I wanted to scribble Sonia's thick crayon over the date above the line holding us together, back and forth across the page the way she used to until it tore a hole in the paper. I knew that if we didn't have children together, I'd have nothing to do with him again. But if I did that and removed the line, the two little circles attached to it on the genogram would be left suspended in mid-air.

Alone in the lounge room that night, after Sonia and Olivia were asleep, the wedding ring resisted my yanking. In forcing it, more skin conspired against me. I persevered and it hurt to twist it to navigate the folds on my knuckle. I placed the ring on the solid, wooden coffee table often used as an impromptu dance floor at parties. More recently it had become Sonia's drawing table. Off my finger, the ring looked empty. It sat amongst the table's red wine circles and Sonia's Texta loops. A foolish band of white remained on my finger. As soon as Sonia woke up the next morning, she noticed. Her head fell to one side, like a puppy hearing a new sound. 'Mummy, where's your beautiful ring? Let's look for it.' The ring slid back on my finger, more easily than it had been removed.

*

Andrew and I were seated in low, soft armchairs that didn't allow for quick exits. The chairs were placed equidistant either side of a circular coffee table – no sharp edges. The room was arranged the way we were taught to prepare a room: to make clients feel comfortable enough to disclose. This arrangement gives the impression that you are sitting in a friend's lounge room. As a client, I saw how this informality might imply the session was just a casual chat – not acknowledging the gravity of the situation that a more formal arrangement might.

It is said in my profession that the biggest mistake couples make is waiting too long before seeking help. I probably waited longer than most because I *was* a social worker. I could accept that teachers continue to learn and doctors get sick, but I had subconsciously separated social worker and client into mutually exclusive categories. I offered help; I didn't ask for it. I didn't want to tell my story instead of listening to someone else's. I didn't want to use the box of tissues instead of supplying it. I didn't want to be the subject of the genogram instead of the one drawing it. Where families can be proud of their family trees developed in feudal times for select families as proof of their good breeding, genograms tend to show a family's private shames and remain hidden inside a file marked 'confidential'. I wanted to be proud of my family tree, not to be the subject of such a file.

I couldn't see a solution to our problem. I had wholeheartedly believed in marriage. I had whole heartedly believed in the value of knowledge to solve problems, but my evidence-based understanding of human behaviour was not helping me.

Drawing families seemed like a useful skill for a social worker, like knowing Roman numerals – once learned, never forgotten. But my memory for Roman numerals has only proved useful for deciphering those symbols at the end of movies to determine the year it was made. So too, with genograms. One thing I wish I had known before joining with a lifelong partner, was that it could be so very lonely in a marriage.

The children and I had come to be mostly in the home, as Andrew had increasingly spent time away from it. The outline of Andrew's square began to look distant and faded. The line connecting us had become looser and shakier, like elastic gone bung. I'd even caught myself fantasising about what great fathers various members of The Wiggles might make. It was clear from the behaviour around me at Sonia's first Wiggles concert that many other mothers had similar thoughts. As with most bands, it was the front man who demanded my attention.

The counselling session allowed small, bright moments of honesty to crack through the bullshit. It became clear how much effort he had expended over time, a new lie to cover the first and a more intricate one to cover the last. If I spotted a flaw in his story, he'd resort to pushing me. Push me to shut me out. Push me to shut me up. Push me until I stopped asking. Police say that many women endure as many as thirty-five assaults before they make a complaint to them. I didn't keep count. I had, however, begun to email a friend who lived interstate, who I knew I could trust with such information, each time Andrew pushed me or hurt me. The emails were brief and I asked her to delete them when she received them. I didn't want evidence; I just had to go through the process of telling someone, to acknowledge that it truly was happening again and again. It helped because I knew she wouldn't judge me and because she lived interstate I didn't have to face her or talk about it. I felt so ashamed for being in this situation and sadness and concerned for my children. What I hadn't considered was how this must have burdened my friend.

Now Andrew's secret behaviour was like a carcinogenic scab on our genogram. He wanted me to let this scab heal over, but I picked and picked at it with questions. I wanted to see the pink flesh that lay beneath. Before this my questions had led to lies, so many lies, it was exhausting to dig for the truth. Over the previous months, his responses to my questions had been so carefully worded that, to his ears, they probably sounded like truths – 'out with a work colleague', and 'staying at a friend's house'.

In our case, a genogram had not proven to be a tool for assessing risk. My family was the happy 'fertile and stable' one and with Andrew's family as well, there had been no broken or shaky lines. More importantly, genograms can only represent the reality that people are prepared to disclose and they are monochromatic; there is no scale from yellow to red to indicate level of risk,

Risk, however, was on my mind when I was younger and planned to travel overseas. Friends, family and strangers endlessly warned me about being robbed or kidnapped, so I stayed on heightened alert and wore my bag facing the front and limited the places I would go and limited going out at night or on my own. Family and friends ensured they mentioned terrorism, malaria, bilharzia and flesh-eating spiders that lay their eggs just under the skin, so that when they popped open thousands of spiders would run across the victim's face. No one at any point warned me of the risks of entering a relationship and having children – no one. I began to see that falling in love and having children was the riskiest thing I'd ever done. I couldn't trust my husband and I was not safe in my own home. On top of that I had been forced to not trust my own judgement.

Only when I became a client did I begin to understand the internal heaviness a person drags into the social worker's office when their buttocks grip the seat. I began to understand the dense fog in people's brains when the social worker leans forward with the opener, delivered in a calm and caring tone, 'So, (insert name) tell me why you've come today?'

A box of tissues positioned between us was the only hint as to the messy business conducted in that room. The tissue box made its way closer to my side of the table during the hour. I spun the band on my finger constantly, as if it were itching. Andrew spoke only when prompted. The expectation I placed on the social worker for wisdom was beyond human capacity.

'I expected our relationship would be equal,' I said.

I thought the social worker would support me on this but instead she looked alarmed.

'Had you both agreed to that?'

'Was equality something that needed to be agreed to?'

I thought equality, like honesty, was fundamental to a marriage. I recalled then another gem of knowledge from our social work profession: couples that enter marriage with low expectations are happiest. I wondered just how low those expectations needed to be.

'Stay in the marriage or leave,' the social worker said, as if it was that simple.

I imagined the social worker drawing our genogram as a square and a circle joined by a straight line on her notepad. Her pen, like a weapon, could cut the marriage line with a perpendicular one to indicate a separation. This perpendicular line meant events could go either way. Couples could get back together and the wound could be erased. Or a perpendicular line next to the existing one could sever the connection, showing divorce. I imagined the social worker holding the pen ominously above the straight line.

I squeezed the band of gold against my finger and noticed a thick callous on the palm just below it.

The room gulped.

Duct Tape for the Soul

We separated. We continued with counselling. He promised to get counselling about his abusive behaviour. We rearranged our work to spend quality time together as a family. He moved back in, things did improve, but it wasn't easy. Two more years of my life were spent trying to trust again and trying to forgive and start something new.

When Olivia turned three, a work opportunity opened for Andrew overseas. I was proud of him for his achievements. We decided to start a new life in a new country and leave our problems in their country of origin. I agreed to leave my friends, family, my lecturing work at university and the consultancy business for the dream that had always been the most important to me, that of a happy family.

The opportunity was in Los Angeles, of all places. As it turned out, the visas to live and work in the United States were dispatched as the twin towers fell in New York. I decided not to go, then I agreed to go, but we delayed our departure. We eventually found ourselves being photographed, fingerprinted, searched and sniffed as we entered a country that was still in shock and deep in fear and mourning.

Andrew travelled to Los Angeles a month before us to establish himself in his new job and find a place for us to live. In Australia, I sold our furniture, emptied our house and prepared our daughters for the changes.

When we arrived, Andrew proudly showed us the highlights of our new city. It was an odd assortment: a marina with an impressive aquarium; the historic luxury passenger liner, the *Queen Mary*, and a Russian submarine. Then we passed less remarkable parts: gas plants larger than football fields, rusty 'nodding donkeys' that creaked as they continually pulled oil to the surface from under the ground, and offshore oil rigs along the ocean breakwater. Andrew summarised for us what was already clear: 'A cauldron of trapped volatile energy bubbled below us.'

Plaques in downtown Long Beach commemorating an earthquake that had destroyed much of the city in the 1933 ensured we knew the destruction that could happen at any moment. I began to question the wisdom of setting up house so close to the San Andreas Fault as a way to build stability in the marriage. I remembered the statistic that half of all marriages in America end in divorce, but in California it is sixty percent.

The area Andrew chose for us to live in was an extended stretch of Californian coast – aptly named Long Beach. Our apartment was parallel to the beach, five streets back. Built in the 1950s mood of optimism and expansion, it wasn't hard to imagine our apartment block in its heyday. In the egg-shaped pool, where our children would play Marco Polo and accidently do wee wees, I imagined debonair Pan Am pilots and curvy flight attendants once floated on airbeds and sipped margaritas between flights from Long Beach airport.

Los Angeles delivered consistently perfect weather: blue skies, never too cold, never too hot, and never humid. But to my eyes, more accustomed to the sharper Sydney light, it looked like there was a layer of dust over everything. I remember thinking when we arrived that the smog might clear after a few days, but it never did. To add to my dislocation, eucalypts grew on every street, but they didn't resemble the free-range eucalypt that spread across our backyard with no respect for a neighbour's fence line. The eucalypts around our new home were tamed by topiary.

In our first few months in California, the Homeland Security Advisory Service moved the national threat level from yellow to orange – 'elevated risk' to 'high risk' – and sometimes to red. In my house, despite my optimism for change, I, too, held suspicions based on previous behaviour, that the level of threat inside our house hovered between yellow and orange. Police car sirens passed, often as one continuous howl the length of their journey, unlike the sirens back home that took a breath in between. The sound of urgent rotating helicopter blades also penetrated our house as they patrolled the coast. It felt as if they were surveilling our home. It was in the news that phone 'chatter' was intercepted by intelligence agencies, and I, too, became suspicious of Andrew's phone 'chatter', if it was conducted just out of earshot.

Just as we'd begun to settle, the Department of Homeland Security urged Americans to take steps to prepare for a possible terrorist attack. They advised all to cover windows with plastic sheeting, to be held in place with duct tape. I doubted how effective this would be in the case of a terrorist attack, but panic-buying of duct tape and plastic sheeting set in at every Home Depot store, depleting stocks on the shelves.

It made me think about 'duct taping my soul'. It was the social worker who had suggested it: that I do something I enjoyed that was just for me. I certainly hadn't done this since becoming a mother, but I had more time now as Olivia had started preschool. I decided to join a writing group. I tried to create a story by pulling something from my imagination, but elements of my own story kept flowing into the work. Although reluctant to tell my story to friends or family, I seemed compelled to write about it. I didn't care for escaping into science fiction or fantasies.

In my reading, I looked for stories about women who had experienced what I had, to draw from their wisdom and be inspired by their creativity. Sure, there were millions of blogs and Facebook and Instagram posts about motherhood and each woman's unique experience of it, but I wanted to see our experiences reflected in the literary landscape. Sections of bookstores were devoted to books telling mothers what they should do, but there was not the same number of books in which mothers wrote about what they did, or how they felt about it. I joined the local Belmont Shore library just as Federal laws were passed requiring libraries to disclose to the government, if requested, the list of books individuals had borrowed. I hadn't realised that writing and reading could be such dangerous activities.

At Olivia's preschool orientation, Olivia's teacher, Mrs Sanchez – dressed in primary colours – smiled and handed me a blue piece of paper and a black permanent marker.

'We ask all our wonderful parents to write a comfort note for their child.'

'What's a comfort note?'

'You write something that we can read to your daughter to cheer her up when we're in lockdown.'

'Why would you go into lockdown?'

She smiled, I think, at my quaintness. 'We go into lockdown if there's an earthquake, or fire, or a shooter on campus, or a terrorist attack.'

The Positivity of Americans

Despite the difficulties the country was facing at that time, the positive spirit Americans are famous for persevered, and that positivity proved infectious. It led us to buy a new car – a white Chevy Lumina – from a salesman wearing cowboy boots and a snakeskin belt.

The positivity of Americans led us to change our behaviours in many ways. In true Californian style, we started playing beach volleyball. We took to high-fiving after each set, like those around us. 'Good job' became part of our vernacular. When someone missed the ball, but they happened to be standing in the right spot, it was the custom to say, 'Way to be there', with no sarcasm intended, and we took to that, too.

We noticed as well that, in America, if you complimented a parent about their child – 'Your child has good manners', for example – the parent responded with, 'Yes, thank you.' To cynical Australian ears, this sounded like a parent taking too much credit for their child's behaviour. We were used to hearing something that neutralised such a compliment: 'He/she is not like that at home.' But we began to see our usual approach as essentially a putdown in response to a compliment about a child, so we tried to be more positive about that too.

American positivity had inflated my hopes for our relationship, too. Despite the optimism I knew the risks. I was hopeful for a fresh start, but it was also a last chance.

It was in the butterfly enclosure in Exposition Park that it began to look to me as though the risks I had taken had been worth it. That day, inside a large mesh tent, I watched Andrew as he guided our daughters along a path of soothing jasmine and lemon blossom scents. He tiptoed in his black Doc Martins to avoid stepping on a basking spotted buckeye. In the back of the garden a steady trickle of water flowed to a meditative rhythm. He reappeared as the original nerdy but fun science guy I had fallen for many years before.

There was a communal rush of excitement when someone spotted a butterfly, especially one as bright as an orange Julia butterfly, despite knowing the butterflies were prisoners trapped inside the netting. A monarch butterfly, with wings that resembled a Tiffany lamp, fleetingly covered a flower, only to give way to the yellow-and-black-striped zebra longwing – that's what Sonia called it and Andrew confirmed that she was correct.

I had only learned of Andrew's affinity with butterflies on our farewell visit to his family in Queensland. It was then I saw the extensive butterfly collection he had created in his teens that had remained at his parents' house. I liked the image I had of him as a lanky youth furtively chasing butterflies with a net or a bug catcher amongst the agapanthus in his parents' garden. But later, I thought how he must have asphyxiated these harmless creatures with ethyl acetate, painstakingly spreading their fragile wings and pinned them to a board using his mother's sewing pins. Then he'd have methodically typed the butterfly's species one letter at a time on a Dymo label printer to display it inside the glass case.

The butterfly enclosure stood in a crack of green between Downtown Los Angeles and the South Figueroa Corridor, behind the Los Angeles Museum of Natural History. It's not the most salubrious address, but it is part of a large park area that also boasts the 1984 Olympic Games Memorial Colosseum. At the centre of the park was a fountain set inside an extensive rose garden, where young Mexican-American women pose for photographs in spectacular white dresses for their Holy Communion, *quinceañera*, or wedding. The base of this fountain, and seemingly every other fountain in America, was covered with pennies thrown in the belief that wishes come true. I thought about the wishes these young women might have, and the wishes my daughters might have, and the wishes I once had. Before we'd entered the butterfly enclosure, I'd handed some pennies to Sonia and Olivia. Together we made sincere wishes on our pennies before we threw them into the fountain on the count of three.

For some reason my daughters thought they should go to the butterfly pavilion dressed as butterflies. Olivia had been excited to wear the purple furry antennae she'd received as a present and her matching butterfly wings. Each morning when Olivia woke, her first words were, 'Blue shorts and green t-shirt', or whatever she wanted to wear that day, as if she had spent the night dreaming about her wardrobe. The large, wire-framed butterfly wings meant that she resembled one unusually large bug. Sonia was wearing a pair of jeans and a T-shirt that featured a flower print. She also wore her butterfly wings, which were orange.

Instead of antennae, on Sonia's head was a blue hat, the type Australian school children wear each day to protect them from the sun. I had recently started a business introducing American schoolchildren to wearing these hats. In recent years, I'd watched my pale-skinned mother suffer as she had skin cancers cut out from all over her body, and I didn't want that fate for my children, but I had not planned to start an online wholesale business six months into arriving in California – far from it.

Hats had, in fact, been banned in Californian schools because gang members were identified by the colour of the baseball hat they wore at school which had led to violence. The ban had been lifted in the local school district just before we arrived, because a former student died of melanoma not long after finishing school. I hadn't known all this when I mentioned to another mother that children wore hats at school in Australia. One thing led to another and the principal agreed to the wearing of sunhats on the proviso that I source the hats. I didn't anticipate this to be a problem.

There were, in fact, many problems. In a country full of baseball caps, there were no suppliers of hats designed for children's heads that met UV-protection standards. I would have to import them in bulk and to do that I would have to start a business. So, swept up with the can-do attitude of those around me, I did exactly that.

No one knew that starting the sun protection business might offer another form of protection for myself and my daughters if needed. Buying hats had been a very complex way of securing some of the funds from my previous work in Australia which I did not feel I could secure for myself in any other way. The hat business meant I had a source of income that I could control and hats could be sold for money if needed for a quick escape. I'm sure no one could understand how I thought that a warehouse of hats might form a safety

The Positivity of Americans

raft if needed, but I alone was aware of the precariousness of my situation.

*

Andrew helped the girls to find chrysalises they called 'butterfly changing rooms', from which a butterfly would emerge wet and fresh from a chrysalis. Sonia and Olivia had to be encouraged to stand still so that a butterfly would land on them. Olivia took the advice to stand still literally, adopting the statue pose, with her eyes enlarged and her teeth clenched. Only when a butterfly rested on the hem of her shorts did she again take a breath. When a butterfly chose to rest on the flower on Sonia's T-shirt, she called everyone over to see it, including a bride who had entered the enclosure for wedding photos and competed with the butterflies for visitor attention.

An attendant at the butterfly enclosure drew our attention to a luna moth about to hatch on a passionfruit vine. The 'moff', as Sonia called it through a missing front tooth, pushed through the chrysalis with slow determination. He was a velvety white, which we watched transform to a light green as he began to blend in with his surroundings. He began to unfurl his wet wings. On his head were two thick, black, furry feelers. Then he started to shake his body, and we could hear a low hum as he revved up.

'He doesn't have a mouth because all the food he needs is stored in his body,' the attendant explained. 'He only has one week of food, so he has to find a mate in that time, or he won't have a family.'

Sonia and Olivia gasped. Andrew then took over the narration of the luna moth story. He lightened his tone and presented the story of the moth as if it were a television soap opera: 'The stakes are high, the future generations of luna moths depend on this one moth stepping up and doing everything right in a very short space of time.'

Andrew looked to me and raised his eyebrows, clearly acknowledging the parallels of the moth's situation with his own. 'Can he do it?' he asked with his eyes locked on mine.

Sonia, not understanding the subtext, picked up on the fun and joined in, 'Go, moffie! You can do it!'

'Go moffie!' Olivia echoed.

I listened as Andrew dramatised the moth's life cycle as he walked with the girls. His hair had returned to its earthy brown and his shirts had returned to plain colours.

In the afternoon, Andrew and I sat on a garden bench and watched our children wait for more moths to emerge. We folded into one another like butterfly wings. Eventually, the children joined us on our laps, sitting sideways with their wings sticking out behind them. We remained like this long after the last bride left and the luna moth took his first unsteady flight. Butterflies stopped to rest on us. In the dappled light of the afternoon, our still-entwined bodies must have looked to the attendants like very strange brightly patterned creatures.

Verbraekennisation

After eighteen months of preschool, Olivia moved to Miss Saunders' kindergarten classroom at Fremont Elementary, Long Beach, California, USA, Planet Earth.

In Miss Saunders' classroom, the life cycle of a butterfly was presented as stages around a circle – eggs, larvae, caterpillar and butterfly. The human life cycle was illustrated in a similar way – birth, childhood, adulthood and death. On this diagram, each stage of human life looks to be given an equal amount of time. In Miss Saunders' classroom, however, childhood was rushed. It felt like children were running out of time in this stage in order to reach the next. The classrooms were dynamic and fast paced. Clocks and calendars were as ubiquitous as American flags. There were words made from Lego, number stickers and letters made of calico for children to draw designs on with colourful markers. Numbers and letters popped off walls and dangled from the ceiling like spiders, so that even the most reticent student might accidentally bump into learning.

Childhood was built from moments stacking on moments like brightly coloured blocks, each moment building on the next and each too quickly lost. Each moment was a learning opportunity not to be wasted, even waiting in line to go home. I knew this because on Mondays I was a parent helper in the classroom. I had the role of pointing at the sight words tacked to the wooden door frame as the children exited in single file. My role was to listen to each child read the words, and correct any strugglers before they could go to collect their schoolbag. I felt the end-of-the-day excitement pulsing from body to body down the line: 'they', 'this', 'from' 'with'.

Olivia's teacher, Miss Saunders, appeared to be an enchantress. Despite her habit of speaking to parents as if they were children, and her lack of understanding that a microphone does the work of amplifying voice, making it unnecessary for her to shout at school events, she made the illiterate literate, and turned finger-counters into mathematicians. For Olivia, night could only follow day if her teacher said so.

Time inside Olivia's classroom appeared on a round wooden clock with red plastic hands that only moved with teacher assistance. It was the exact same style of clock I remembered from when I was at school. Olivia's school insisted on teaching a concept of time that children just didn't have. Children's time is the present moment. Parents know this because we are tasked with counting the number of sleeps until birthdays, holidays and other occasions.

Children gnaw away at time. I was often trying to steal a morsel of it for myself. How things had changed, from when I was a child, when time was plentiful. In those days, time wasn't precious, it was free for all citizens, like education and healthcare. By calling the free number 1194 you could hear the movement of time. People used this service to set their analogue watches. A proper English voice announced, 'On the third stroke it will be…' followed by what I assumed was

Verbraekennisation

Big Ben bonging from London. Each minute was infinite, like my childhood. I spent it waiting – waiting for parents to finish talking, or cooking, or shopping, or mowing the lawn, or watching TV. Waiting for Christmas or my birthday, waiting to start school, waiting to start high school, waiting to be old enough to drive, or drink or vote.

I can't imagine how it is for my children; I don't think that they have been given the luxury of time that I had as a child, their lives are already at tomorrow. The four- and five-year-olds in Miss Saunders' class were expected to work beyond their grade level (Kindergarten) and were rewarded for it.

When Sonia had attended preschool in Australia, we had the choice of small, local community-run preschools in converted houses that featured rainbows or teddy bears on their logos. Over time, The Rainbow Room and Smile Preschool had been replaced by Little Achievers and First Grammar Preschool held in large commercial enterprises in buildings resembling office blocks. These institutions had no grassed play area, but advertised that they offered security and surveillance. The logos of smiling teddy bears and rainbows had given way to a stack of books and mortarboards. This reflected a change in focus from the whole child's development through play, to one centred on intellectual development through supervised study, as early as possible.

This approach to education reminded me of my childhood friend, Tanya Verbraekenn, and her family. Our friendship had been forged early in Year 3 when Tanya generously offered me unfettered use of her equally sized Derwent pencils to colour the title pages of my schoolbooks. These pencils were a luxury product in our school. They came in colours that stretched beyond the rainbow and they softly touched the page, leaving a smooth layer, rather than the harsh, single-pointedness of the cheaper pencils of various lengths lying in my Snoopy pencil case. If you owned Derwents or a complete set of *World Book* encyclopaedias, your circle of friends grew at assignment time. I owned neither, but when I was in Year 3 at Punchbowl Primary, Tanya was the child nobody wanted to be. I found out why when I went to her house for a play date. It began well enough. Tanya's father took us to Roselands pool, where we swam for a while but left famished. Her father seemed immune to the beckoning smell of hot chips sold at the entrance. Our rounded bellybuttons peeked out between the top and bottom of our bikinis, like eyes looking for food. I was relieved to see glistening watermelon cut into what Tanya called obtuse triangles when we arrived back at her house.

We sat at the kitchen table, but I was stopped midway through reaching for a piece of watermelon by Mrs Verbraekenn, standing in the kitchen in a floral dress.

'When you answer a question, you can have some watermelon,' she announced like a schoolteacher.

I was used to friends who said grace before they ate, but I'd never been to a house where you had to answer questions before eating. This didn't concern me too much at first. I knew the answers to the limited range of questions adults asked: 'How old are you now?', 'What does your father do for work?' and 'What do you want to do when you grow up?'

Without instruction, Tanya rose from her seat and moved to the wall behind me, like a trained animal. I had been so focused on the watermelon on the table in front of me that I hadn't noticed the world map pasted across the kitchen wall behind me. I'd never seen a map of the world on a kitchen wall; in fact, I'd rarely seen a map of the world. This was a time when encyclopaedias were the internet. Googling was not an option; you had to wait until information was presented to you. Teachers and librarians were the respected holders of knowledge and they administered it to us in small, age-relevant doses, like immunisation. We caught a glimpse of Africa or Europe as maps of pastel-coloured continents unrolled for our edification, but we were not considered mature enough in Year 3 to see the world.

'Can you name the highest mountain in the world?' Mr Verbraekenn asked Tanya. That was not the sort of question I was expecting. I was scared for Tanya, but I shouldn't have been. Tanya threw her father a look that said, 'Really, Dad, do you think I'm in kindergarten?' Then she said a word that sounded like it could have been a brand of pillows or toothpaste, for all I knew:

'Everest.'

I was sure she'd made it up, but her father looked pleased and instructed her to point to it.

What sort of family was this?

It made me realise how normal my own family was, after all. I wished I was back in my family kitchen eating Froot Loops.

Without hesitation, Tanya confidently pointed to some yellow area in a tangle of different-coloured countries.

'Very good, you can now have some watermelon,' her father said.

Mr Verbraekenn then turned to me. I felt something like the feeling I used to get when we had maths mental tests first thing every Friday.

'Now, Lynn, please stand.'

I looked across to Tanya for support, but she was devouring her juicy obtuse triangles.

'Lynn, you must name and point to the highest mountain in Australia, and then you can have some watermelon, too.'

I sensed he was giving me what he thought was an easy question. At least I knew what Australia looked like. I stood up and headed towards Australia on the map. But Australia was all brown and flat with no mountains sticking up, and it was big, really big. I scanned it, but couldn't find an area labelled 'mountain' or even 'hill'. I knew of the Great Dividing Range but it was long, not high. Tanya offered no hints. In my panic, it came to me. It made complete sense, right in the middle of Australia. Where else would you put the biggest mountain? I felt so confident I could almost feel the cool, sugary watermelon juices sliding down my chin as I bit into the soft, crunchy flesh.

'Ayers Rock!' I proclaimed loudly as my finger pushed into the map like a pioneer who thought he was the first to discover what I would later come to learn was Uluru.

I don't remember exactly what happened after that. There was laughter and disbelief and pointing all over Australia and mention of 'snow'. Eventually, I was given a piece of watermelon. It wasn't cold, or juicy or crunchy.

At the end of that year, Tanya and I went our separate ways. Tanya attended the Opportunity Class and I was left wondering what the Opportunity Class was. What I did know that day as my eight-year-old-self, was that Mr Verbraekenn should have just let Tanya and I play and fed us when we were hungry. What I instinctively knew then was that play and joy and friends and food are just as important as knowing the tallest mountain. What I could not express then but I know now is that a child's social and emotional intelligence is just as important (if not more important) than their intellectual intelligence. They all go hand in hand.

Despite instinctively feeling at a young age that 'Verbraekennising' children wasn't right, as my own children grew older, especially once they started school, I felt the pressure to Verbraekennise them. I felt the pressure to value and privilege their intellectual development above their social and emotional development. I felt the pressure to coerce my children into achieving at every moment; it was a movement building amongst parents all around me and it was easy to be swept up in it.

If Andrew's job opportunity had arisen in Finland rather than the United States, Olivia and her friends would not have been graded until they were seven. My daughters wouldn't have had homework until high school and they would only have sat a standardised test once when they were sixteen. Their teachers would have been valued for the important work they do and been paid accordingly. My children would have been amongst the children of Finland who have consistently scored the highest on international tests. It looks like the Finns don't Verbraekennise their children and it pays off for them.

*

As a parent, I've thought a lot about my children's childhoods. When I studied psychology, I learned that childhood is the most significant time in life influencing future development. At the same time, in sociology, I was introduced to the idea that a childhood as such does not even exist. That is, children are real, but childhoods are ideals. Not every child around the world has a childhood the way that I had a childhood, or my children have a childhood. Many children around the world work rather than attend school. In some countries today children are exploited as cheap labour, sometimes soldiers, even sex workers.

Over the centuries, children in western societies have been viewed in a variety of ways. At one time they were seen as innocents requiring protection, at another time as little devils requiring punishment. They have been used as chimney sweeps, coal miners and textile factory workers. Social, economic, political and religious forces have historically influenced how children are viewed and how they should be raised.

In the museums I had visited with Andrew across America for his work, I had seen many exhibits depicting human development. They inevitably show the profile of an ape-man scraping his knuckles through the mud, slowly unfolding as if from a yoga pose over millennia to stand upright, through Neanderthal and Cro-Magnon, to become the intellectual Homosapien. Human development: an enlarging brain, learning to walk, losing body hair, using tools. The evolution diagrams often stop at contemporary man as if evolution ends with us. Similarly, if children are the *next* generation, are we claiming that we are *the* generation? Adults tend to emphasise children's futures more than their present. The question most asked of my children is, 'What do you want to do when you grow up?' It's as if they are not thought of as still becoming someone rather than being someone.

Freud, Piaget and Kohlberg conceived of biological theories of child development that every teacher, social worker, psychologist and advertiser has studied. Each theory allocates time to children in stages, during which a set outcome should be achieved. They theorise that problems happen if a child's development does not follow a predetermined path. But even these once well-established theories of child development have been shaken up over the years.

Lawrence Kohlberg's stages of moral development theory, for example, has influenced courts to determine at what age a child could reason about right and wrong and be tried or imprisoned for a crime. This understanding of child development has influenced why many children can be imprisoned in Australia, even as young as ten. Kohlberg was a psychologist who conducted experiments with children in the 1960s to determine at what ages they develop moral values. He concluded that justice was universally the highest moral value, that is, that following the letter of the law was the right thing. Kohlberg, however, didn't think to conduct his experiments with girls.

Twenty years later, psychologist Carol Gilligan conducted the same experiments with girls and found that for girls, the highest moral value was not justice, but to care for others. She found that girls considered context and relationships, (such as if someone was dying and needed medicine, or was starving and needed to eat) to be more important than following the rules. Her work overturned some established views on child development. It also sparked the concept of an ethics of care. An ethics of care argues that caring work is core to every society. We all need care at some time in our lives and someone needs to provide that. That someone is usually a woman and mostly this work is unpaid and unrecognised. Gilligan suggests that an ethics of care framework, rather than a legal rights framework, might create a better society. In such a society, the importance of care would be rewarded appropriately. If this were the case, the valuable work of parenting would be recognised and caring professions such as childcare workers, social workers, nurses and teachers would not be amongst the poorest-paid university-educated people.

In Miss Saunders' kindergarten classroom at Fremont Elementary, Long Beach, California, USA, Planet Earth, there is a poster on the wall of a First Nations American silhouetted against a sunset. On it is written a quote attributed to Chief Seattle: '*We do not inherit the earth from our ancestors, we borrow it from our children.*'

The Happiest Place on Earth

I was trapped inside the happiest place on earth when I realised that the positivity of Americans might not be enough to save our marriage.

After a bag search, we passed through turnstiles that made the sound of Tinkerbell's magic wand. Once inside the park, we were handed a map. Sonia took one look at it and yelled, 'Princess castle!'

'Princess castle!' Olivia repeated.

Sleeping Beauty's castle was easy to find, as the central landmark of the theme park. Andrew and I thought we'd seen something like it before. We had! It was inspired by the best-known castle in the world – Neuschwanstein in Bavaria. Whereas Neuschwanstein is large, Sleeping Beauty's castle makes use of 'forced perspective', an architectural device that makes it appear taller than it actually is.

We discovered from the map that Disneyland is like a country, divided into different lands, such as Adventureland and Tomorrowland. Sleeping Beauty's castle was rightly situated in Fantasyland. To reach Fantasyland, we had to help our children resist the smell of popcorn and corndogs as we walked the 'Main Street' full of Mickey Mouse shops and then crossed a moat.

The castle was dimly lit. It hosted a small shop selling make-believe with a big price tag. Inside, tiny 'want-to-be princesses' wore polyester princess gowns, tiaras and plastic shoes with impossible heels. Sonia and Olivia were jealous that they were not allowed to join in the purchasing frenzy.

Outside the castle, a number of 'real' princesses were signing autographs, including Sleeping Beauty, with her Fairy Godmother, and Cinderella. Sonia and Olivia were besotted. When Cinderella left, another princess arrived dressed in a golden-yellow gown that flounced like a Southern belle's. She was the princess from *Beauty and the Beast.* Her lavish red curls fell over the scoop neck of her gown. Sonia and Olivia yelled out, 'Belle!' as they ran to her, jostling other girls in the hope of an autograph. I wasn't prepared for autographs, but along with tissues, Band-Aids, wet wipes and my phone, paper and pen was something I always had in my 'mother bag'. When we were close, I realised I had met her before. She had a son in Sonia's class at school. I could tell Sonia was confused that real mums could be real princesses and that real princesses could be real mums.

The woman acting as the princess Belle and I had previously struck up a conversation in the playground, waiting for our children to finish school one day. On that day, she wore denim shorts with Ugg boots so I knew she had a tattoo that snaked up one of her legs and slid along one arm. The golden ball gown covered the tail of the snake on her leg and the long golden gloves covered the head on her arm.

Belle signed her autograph using a loose, loopy calligraphy dotted with a love heart above the B. There were no other children around Belle at that time, so I introduced Andrew, who then greeted her with, 'G'day.' I'd never heard him say 'g'day' in his life. Andrew generally used formal speech and was highly articulate, with a clipped, private school voice, but ever since he'd dressed as Steve Irwin, Crocodile Hunter, for our first American Halloween, he'd begun to speak with a broad 'Strayan accent. Talking with Belle, he began to pepper his conversation with 'mate'. I threw him what I intended to be a playful look of astonishment.

Belle told us how the Disney princesses attend autograph school to learn to sign their autograph. This way the autograph is consistent regardless of who plays the character each day.

'At Disneyland, every day is a performance,' she said. 'Visitors are guests, and employees are cast members. What guests can see is onstage – anywhere they can't see is backstage.'

Eventually Belle attracted a new throng of children, so we left.

'What's with the fake Australian accent?' I asked Andrew.

'Stop nagging,' he said audibly, followed less audibly with the word, 'bitch.' Despite it being barely audible, it carried with it a force that blew across my face and onto our children. I saw their shock and then their quick recovery. Passers-by turned to look. Hearing it out in the open, I realised Andrew had resumed this way of talking to me at home, too. We were all edgily silent after that.

It was only ten twenty-five in the morning. We had to stay until the 'Believe...there's magic in the stars spectacular' fireworks at nine-thirty at night. We were at Disneyland – we had to enjoy ourselves.

'What ride should we go on?' Andrew asked, as if nothing had happened.

'Tups!' Olivia shouted.

The Cup and Saucer ride was based around the theme of The Mad Hatter's Tea Party from *Alice in Wonderland*. As we walked towards the ride, the Evil Queen from *Snow White* appeared before us. She didn't smile like the other characters. She maintained her evilness and the girls picked up on it; they didn't know how to react. They didn't run towards her as they had with the other characters. Instead, Sonia ran towards me.

'From one evil queen to another,' Andrew said.

I held Sonia close and glared at him.

When we realised Olivia was not big enough for the more thrilling rides, Andrew suggested that he take Sonia to Tomorrowland to ride Space Mountain before the lines grew too long. After that, they'd come back and meet us.

On the Cup and Saucer ride, the more Olivia turned the wheel, the more we spun, so the more Olivia turned the wheel. Her bobbed hair winged out from her head in the breeze created by the centrifugal force. I was feeling a slight nausea. She enjoyed being in control of the wheel and when she took control, she was out of control. We exited the ride a little groggy and sat on the nearby seats. After a while Olivia suggested we go again, so we did. While we waited in line, the unmistakable aroma of sugar and cinnamon sprinkled over hot, fried dough was nipping at our nostrils. So, after the third Cup and Saucer ride, we bought some churros to eat while we waited on a seat for Sonia and Andrew to return. I texted.

'Again?' Olivia suggested.

Back in the queue, Olivia slipped her small hand, rough with grains of sugar, into my hand. When the ride ended, Andrew and Sonia were still nowhere to be seen. I called, no answer. We joined the line for other rides near the Cup and Saucer, keeping an eye out for them. Another hour passed.

Olivia, in front of me in the line, pressed her whole body backwards to rest against mine. I wrapped my arms around her and folded her into me.

Two more times on the Cup and Saucer, then we waited on a bench surrounded by a neat garden where every single flower matched its neighbour in size and colour.

I rang. No answer. We waited. I called again. No answer. We waited. We bought a lemon drink. We finished the drink. We sat, we waited. Olivia grabbed my face in both of her wet, sticky hands and pulled it close to hers. 'Don't worry, Mummy.' Then she pressed her nose upwards with her right middle finger while at the same time pulling down on her cheeks with the fingers on the other hand to reveal her vein-filled eyeballs. This was a performance aimed at diverting my attention and to make me laugh.

We were laughing when Sonia ran up to us.

'Mummy, Mummy, we went on Indiana Jones!'

'Did you? I thought you were going to Space Mountain?'

'Space Mountain was dark and scary!' she said, enlarging her hazel eyes and attempting to grit her missing front teeth.

'Tell Mummy how much fun we had,' Andrew said as he arrived behind Sonia.

Olivia chimed in first: 'We went on Tup and Saucer…'

Sonia replied, 'You went on Cup and Saucer because you're too little to go on Indiana Jones.'

'Am not.'

'Yes, you are.'

'You poopooweeweeheadie!'

I pulled Andrew aside: 'Why didn't you come back after Space Mountain, like we agreed?'

He answered, addressing Sonia. 'We thought we'd just sneak another ride in, didn't we, Sonia?'

'But you left us here waiting for you.'

'Well, we're here now, aren't we, Sonia?'

'But we didn't know where you were or what had happened.'

'Oh, *shut up*!'

'Mummy, we went to Adventureland!'

'You poopooweeweeheadie!'

'Am not!'

Andrew had gone to Adventureland and Tomorrowland and left me stuck in Fantasyland.

*

The girls wanted to conquer Splash Mountain, a popular ride that peaked above the park, so we pushed on to Frontierland. Andrew and I were still engaged in bouts of silence interspersed with snipes passed only within earshot. Sonia and Olivia responded as if they, too, had forgotten their public etiquette, pulling and swinging on the ropes that corralled the queue of families into sections.

After ninety minutes in line, all four of us were seated one behind the other on plastic seats moulded and painted to resemble a log. I was not comforted by the lack of safety belts. I worried Olivia might fall out. On safer rides, I had wrapped myself around her, using my body as her seatbelt. She was in a seat in front of me, but I couldn't move forwards because the slow ascent had begun, and gravity was pulling us backwards. On such rides, my stomach usually tightened in anticipation of a freefall to come, but my stomach was already knotted before I sat down. I closed my eyes. My safety, the safety of all of us, was taken out of my hands for a few seconds – and it was incredibly freeing. The *chunk, chunk, chunk* of the ascent sounded like a giant was on the top of the mountain pulling the cars up by a metal chain.

Suspended.

A camera stationed just before the splash captured the first moment of falling. Everyone around me screamed. I just let the falling happen. Then our log-carriage levelled out and the ride ended with a gentle splash.

The photographs taken at that moment of falling appear at the exit of the ride, so that as you walk past you see your reaction to fear supersized on a digital screen. Sonia and Olivia successfully pestered us to buy our photograph. In it, Andrew's eyes are wide open; mine are closed. Sonia and Olivia have their mouths open in a silent scream, their eyes popping. We are all propelled forward, gripping on tight.

Entrapment

The room was warm and there was just enough light to see people, but not enough to discriminate on details. The clean reverberation of Tibetan singing bowls made the community hall seem more expansive than it was. It smelt of patchouli and sparked a memory of the birth centre where Olivia was born. I hadn't planned for taking shoes off – my toenails had not been attended to for some time. I also disliked the feel of walking on smooth floorboards barefoot, so I walked across the floor of the yoga studio to reach my yoga mat, the way I walk across scorching sand on a beach to reach my towel. A good friend from the writing group, Marlene, and I had left our children with their fathers, and we were planning to make the most of our hour of child-free time. I thought we were going to a gym class, dressed as I was in body-hugging Lycra, but Marlene suggested yoga.

I laid the mat I'd borrowed from Marlene on the floor and spread my body over it like everyone else had done, lying on their backs. Eye closing was encouraged, but I couldn't relax; it just made me conscious of how many thoughts crammed into my head every second. The edges of one thought morphed into another. I looked out of the side of one eye in response to any sound or movement. Lying on the floor in public with strangers was a new experience for me. I needed to constantly adjust my head, my neck and my back. There was tightness in my face, across my shoulders, in my stomach and across my chest. Marlene had her eyes closed, and so I tried to relax, too.

'Let go of attachments,' the yoga instructor said softly. It was as if she had stepped inside my mind and found an immovable cement block. I knew it was hard for me to let go of attachments, but wasn't that a good quality? Wasn't I attached to my children? Shouldn't a marriage be binding? As she continued, it became clear that she wasn't talking about my relationships. She considered every thought and every feeling an attachment that could simply be let go, 'like a cloud floating by'. Could long-established wisdom, evidence-based theories, romantic ideals and good-mother expectations all be let go? Her intention in saying this, I assumed, was to stop our minds wandering, but this had the opposite effect on mine.

My mind was focused on the previous day, when I'd taken the girls to Andrew's work, the La Brea Tar Pits and Museum. The museum is famous for its skeletons of ice age animals that prospectors unearthed when they began drilling for oil there in the early 1900s. Sabre-toothed cats, Colombian mammoths, sloths, dire wolves and mastodons buried for forty thousand years presented themselves to prospectors along with oil. Remarkably, this prehistoric site on the Wiltshire Boulevard is ten minutes down the road from the handprints and footprints of movie stars along the Hollywood Walk of Fame.

It is believed the animals became stuck when they entered what looked like a lake, to have a drink, and found themselves trapped in the tar hiding below the water, not knowing that in the Ice Age a layer of water had flowed across the area of thick tar. Immobilised, they would have looked like an easy meal for predators, who followed them into the water, to also find themselves stuck in the tar. Then the predator of that predator would be trapped, and so on.

Sonia and Olivia were excited to see their dad at work and to come face to face with the animals they knew from the *Ice Age* movies. The drone of Wiltshire Boulevard traffic faded as we entered the extensive lawns scarred with large, open holes from excavation. To me, they resembled cemetery plots. We found Andrew stomping between the greasy pits in his Doc Martins the way I imagine a butcher moves through a blood-filled abattoir.

We had planned to have a picnic with Andrew during his lunchbreak. I spread out a blanket and began to pull out containers of carrot sticks, celery sticks, olives, salami and dips. Sonia and Olivia quickly dipped sticks and ran off, playing stuck in the mud near the tar pits surrounding us. In the large tar-filled lake nearby, the moment of entrapment of a mother mammoth and her baby is re-enacted in life-sized fibreglass figures. It did require some imagination to see these smooth white replicas as woolly mammoths. The majestic mother mammoth is trapped up to her belly in the vast lake of tar, while the baby, also trapped, looks on helplessly. The mother's strength, her height, her U-shaped tusks rising up in a desperate call for help, are all rendered useless by the black death holding her. In reality, the mother and baby are joined and held in place by a chain that runs through their bodies just below the tar line, rattling eerily as they move. In horror, she is rocked back and forth, from the ice age to the present age, with the real-time movement of the still-bubbling tar beneath them. I found myself moving in rhythm with that mother and her child, the way I used to continue to sway long after the baby I was rocking to sleep had settled in her cot.

In the real time of the yoga class, on mats of all colours, we knelt on all fours in poses the instructor called 'cat' and 'cow', and twisted our upper bodies in actions called 'threading the needle'.

Just as I was noticing the tension between and around my shoulders her calm voice, barely louder than a whisper, said, 'Knots in our bodies are psychological barriers binding the soul – they lock us to our misperception of reality and root us in fear.' It was becoming clear that this was not at all like a gym class.

'When I let go of what I am, I become what I might be, Lao Tzu.'

From then on, we unblocked our limitations by introducing our head to our thighs, hands to ankles and elbows to opposite knees. Although I was holding onto my knots of scepticism and disinterest, I found that with each posture a different region of my body presented itself in an astonishing new way. I found I could make myself into a lion, a cobra or a dog, whatever animal the teacher demonstrated, while staying low on the mat. But once we stood up, I found I had no balance. I couldn't become a tree, a dancer or an eagle. I thought this was odd because I had been a dancer all my life.

'Chakras draw energy to keep the spiritual, mental, emotional and physical health of the body balanced,' she whispered.

She placed her hands just above each of these chakra centres on her own body, beginning at the base of the spine.

'*Muladhara*, the centre for stability. *Swadisthana*, near the ovaries, for sexual energy and creativity. *Manipura*, near the bellybutton, the centre for personal power.'

Slowly, the class followed her lead. I actually began to feel each area pulse as my attention went there. These areas aligned with glands in the body that produce hormones, so it made a lot of sense to me.

'*Anahata*, the heart, the centre of compassion and forgiveness. *Vishuddhi*, in the throat, for clear communication. *Ajna*, the wisdom of the third eye, between the eyebrows. *Sahasrara*, at the crown of the head – enlightenment, represented by the exquisite lotus flower that grows out of the mud.'

My mind wandered back to when the girls played stuck in the mud as Andrew and I sat on the picnic blanket near the tar pits. The smell of the tar reminded me of driving on country roads in Australia when the asphalt from recently filled potholes pings against the car body. It surfaced a memory of our road trip to Gilgandra and the arguments that followed.

'There's no point digging up the past,' he said.

'That's a bit rich coming from a guy who digs up fossils for a living!'

My attention was brought back to the yoga room by a rogue fart that cut the silence during boat pose, *navasana*. Fortunately, it wasn't mine. In shoulder stand, where legs went above heads, sounds could be heard that only mothers who had delivered vaginally knew existed. Marlene and I, like schoolgirls, had to suppress giggles.

I think I groaned when I saw the yoga teacher creating a circle with her body, her feet on the ground near her hands, head upside down facing us like a circus performer.

'Wheel pose – strong heart opener – allows forgiveness.'

I already knew that forgiveness was elusive. I watched those around me moving their bodies like children in a playground. I remembered pushing myself upside down as a child, too. How light I used to feel. I wanted to feel that lightness again. I pushed my weight into my feet as instructed and stretched out my arms, as my hands lay facing backwards on the floor. My heart offered no resistance, as if it were a paper cut-out that children make at school on Valentine's Day. It became the highest point on my body, pushing up to the ceiling. I found myself smiling at the wall behind me. A new perspective. I imagined the circle of energy around my heart, like an electric hotplate switched on, getting hotter and redder and stronger.

My heart wanted to push even higher in this posture. The heat from around my heart was warming the rest of my body. I wanted to stay longer, but after a while an ache shunted across my lower back, so I came down. Even as I lay flat, the hotplate burned.

'Love,' she said to the class, 'is not romance.'

She had my attention.

'Love is the act of turning up each day.'

She was describing my life as a mother. Or was she telling me I should stick at my marriage?

*

In that yoga class, I was unlearning my profession. Bodies were not given much attention in social work. Social workers don't roll around on the ground in loose pants placing their knees around their ears in 'deaf man's pose' and enlivening their chakras; social workers help people by wearing smart-casual clothes, sitting upright and listening. Active listening was a social worker's core skill, helping people to express, control or repackage their emotions. Social workers could treat emotions like criminals to be witnessed, named, assessed, sentenced, released, and if they reoffended, another appointment could be booked. But in the yoga room, it was silence that healed. In that yoga room, a problem didn't need to be a problem, it didn't need to be labelled, it was neither good nor bad, it just was. Problem solving in the yoga studio came not from concentrating on it, but rather from not concentrating on it. Freedom came from not being bound to anything.

These new ideas were taking a while to slide into my upside-down brain, the way a rich meal takes time to dissolve in the intestine. We came down onto our backs. My spine felt like space had opened between each vertebra. It felt like space had opened in my brain too. The yoga instructor invited us to end the class in corpse pose. This did not sound at all appealing. She gave instructions to lie flat, arms alongside the body, palms facing the ceiling, legs wide, feet flopping outwards. I pressed the small of my back into the mat. Out of the side of my eye I saw the teacher silently wrapping other students in thick woven blankets of earthy browns and oranges. It made them look like the Guatemalan worry dolls Olivia and Sonia placed under their pillows. I wasn't cold, but she methodically placed a woollen blanket over my torso, taking the time to cocoon my feet. Then she added another blanket over me and continued to gently tuck the blanket under and along the side of my body, allowing my body to accept the new arrangement, rather than lifting or moving it. I closed my eyes and felt her sealing me with a third blanket.

Lying flat, I felt supported by the ground beneath me and nourished in the oven of blankets above and around me. My body, my skin, my heart, every organ pulsed with the rhythm of a jellyfish. Tears slid down at new angles into my ears and hair. These were not the pear-shaped tears I'd released in the social worker's office; these tears seeped out, like warm honey from a spoon sweetening a medicinal tea.

Bound

As the country we lived in barrelled into a war, I tried to retreat from the one being waged in my own house and get my children to safety.

Sonia and Olivia were strapped in their car seats, compacted by luggage and belongings we would carry on the plane. I left them with their father, in the hire car parked outside the garage at the back of our apartment. It would be a number of weeks until the girls would see him on the other side of the world, so I wanted to give all three of them the time each needed to say their goodbyes. I didn't know where Andrew was going to live back in Sydney, but I knew we would never live in the same house together again. I headed inside the apartment, and as I passed through the lounge room, I noticed that the removal of our family photographs – after only two years – had left ghostly patches on the wall. Without the photographs and the belongings, the apartment no longer looked like a home, but a rental. I headed to the bedroom the girls had shared. Behind the door, ground into the carpet from the door opening and closing, I found a die from a board game that had been left behind. I smiled at the memory of the fun the four of us had had playing Trouble and other board games, especially when Sonia and Olivia didn't understand the rules. I collected the die and placed it in my jeans pocket.

*

In our previous period of optimism, we had planned and booked a holiday at Lake Tahoe to give our daughters the experience of a white Christmas. Tahoe is a popular ski field with snow-filled vistas most Australians only see on Christmas cards. Ice needles hung from chalets, and the snow formed thick, flat layers across branches of ponderosa pines and on our car.

We stayed at the historic Cal Neva Hotel, aptly named because it straddles the border between California and Nevada. In its heyday, Frank Sinatra, Marilyn Monroe and the Kennedys had been guests there. This hotel had an unusual feature. There was a line painted along the wooden floor in the reception area, dividing the two states. It reminded me of an episode of *The Brady Bunch* I had liked when I was a child, where Peter divides the room he shares with Bobby in the same way, by sticking tape along their floor to keep each to their own side. Sharing a bedroom with my sister at the time, I had wanted to do the same thing. There was no smoking or gambling allowed in California, but in Nevada you could do whatever the hell you wanted. On the Nevada side, poker machines and roulette tables were clouded in smoke, and sex workers handed out porn-shot business cards. On that holiday, Andrew metaphorically stayed in Nevada and I stayed with the children in California. It had been Nevada and California with us ever since.

Bound

*

The separation that followed was not like a cord being cut with scissors; it was more like being cut by a blunt butter knife. It left all of us frayed at the end of a tedious untangling of hearts that, in reality, had started years before. The first love that had unravelled was the one that bookended our wedding vows: the love that rejoiced in the truth, always hoped, always persevered. After that, there was a subtle unpicking of companionship. The home-knitted-woolly-jumper love, the knowing and accepting of flabby bits and faults made from a pattern of familiarity, I don't know when that started to show holes. The joint decision-making over the buying of a rug or the placement of a sofa had also lost its fun. The passionate and robust love that produced passionate and robust children dropped a stitch. I don't remember the order of the losses. The partnered routine in the nightly feed-bath-read-bed race became separate events. The retelling of every action, reaction and interaction our children performed that day, which only parents would care to hear, fell silent. Then the communal love was lost – the shared pride at a child's performance or school report. Even in the casting off – that knot – not wanting the children to be hurt – was the most difficult to untangle.

*

When I told him it was over and that I wanted to return to Australia, I had ensured the children were not home. At first, he showed no emotion. Then he said under his breath, 'You won't get a fuckin' cent, bitch!' He shoved me and shoved me and shoved me.

'Stop or I'll call the Police.'

'Go ahead, I want to see you do it.'

For the first time I did it. I picked up the phone and dialled 911, hands shaking, while he stood over me. I expected him to knock the phone out of my hands, but he just watched me dial. Once I had dialled, I couldn't speak. I pressed the button to end the call and fled to the bedroom. He raced after me, and as I dived on the bed, he reached forward and punched my right ankle. Then he left the room, slamming the door as he left. Within minutes, the police arrived even though I hadn't actually made the call. They sieged the lounge room, guns drawn, shouting, 'Does he have a weapon? Does he have a weapon?'

Two officers interviewed us separately. The officer gave me a list of women's refuges. Why should my children and I have to leave our home? Why not him? I told the police I didn't need a refuge; I needed a way to go back to Australia.

The police visit had scared Andrew. There was no more violence, but there was no more respect. In his mouth my name – when no one else was around – had changed from 'Bitch' to 'Cunt'.

I didn't have a job. I didn't know my rights. Even if I had had a way I could move out, I didn't know if that would void our family visas as I had come as Andrew's partner and I was too scared to talk about the violence or ask anyone about our legal status if we separated in America. We had recently uprooted our children and there would be another massive change of location for them as well as the separation. I didn't have money to move out or to fly home. We lived separated in the same house, but we did not make our separation known. I had to handle this double life – separated inside the house, a couple outside of it. This situation proved the most difficult when friends from Australia stayed with us while on their American holiday. Andrew could be in a rage, but if a visitor entered the room or came to the door, he'd appear as welcoming, gregarious and charming as ever. It was only me, who couldn't flip so easily or quickly, who stood confused, silent and weird when people visited. When they left, he would be silent for days, or weeks.

At the same time, his relationship with our daughters continued unchanged. He was a fun dad, making up silly rhymes as he always had, patient when helping them with their homework and reading to them at night.

*

Andrew had also denied me access to money. To get food, I had to use all my ingenuity. Reading had, by necessity, become more of a source of nourishment than ever. The girls enjoyed reading. We'd visit Belmont Shore library, where we could read while looking across the bay, and Barnes and Noble, where there was an endless supply of fresh, inky books. Each week, the school rewarded students with a voucher for a pizza if they read ten books. Pizza was the School District's successful method of improving literacy, even if the side effect was increasing obesity. A pepperoni pizza became Wednesday night's dinner and I noticed that this was the case for many other families, too.

After some enquiries at the bank, I discovered that since we'd been living in America, Andrew had withdrawn almost the exact amount of his salary each week in a number of cash withdrawals, leaving little more than the amount needed to pay the rent and the utility bills. I looked back to the joint account from Australia and found he had been doing this the whole time. We had only ever been living off the money I earned. I understood then why we had never seemed to have enough money, and he had never wanted to make a budget or set joint financial goals. I wondered where he stashed this cash. The girls and I survived on the smallest amounts of money I received for freelance writing or selling hats. I wasn't eating much. Fortunately, the school cafeteria, which Sonia initially misheard as the 'cup-of-tea area', provided hot meals each day for one dollar. We had a supply of black beans, corn and rice that I had bought at Costco to last in the event of an earthquake. Parents often brought in vegetables or fruit they had grown to share and the girls were well fed when playing at other people's houses. When visiting Costco or Trader Joe's, I'd encourage the girls to return to the free samples table many times, where they served cheese and crackers, organic nachos or vegetarian lasagnes, yoghurts and juices. Fortunately, Andrew's director at work, who I had befriended, gave the girls vouchers to buy clothes at The Children's Place for their birthdays and at Christmas.

Before he left for work one morning, I asked Andrew for twenty dollars as a contribution for Sonia's teacher's present for Teacher Appreciation Day. The 'homeroom mom' had a list of names to be ticked off once the contribution had been paid, so I had no way of getting out of it without embarrassing Sonia.

'I don't have any money to give you.'

When I heard his car leave to go to work, I felt into the pockets of his black Levis, left draped over the chair in our room. Tucked into the lining of the corner of the back pocket was a fifty-dollar note. A less astute hand, a hand belonging to someone who had not been forced over time to become a thief of their own money, might have mistaken the tightly folded fifty-dollar note as the unfortunate remains of a receipt, left in the pocket during the wash. But I was familiar with the origami of the greenback, having already found its construction hidden in the corners of coats, wallets and jeans when I was going to wash them. I had come to learn that he couldn't get angry with me for finding these hidden notes, because he had already denied there was any money.

Near the chair, I noticed his 'Little Devil' boxer shorts left lying on the carpet where they had been taken off. I picked them up and held them by the elastic. I gritted my teeth as I found the strength in my pectoral muscles to pull each side of the shorts in opposite directions – 'Hold, one two three' – as if working out in a gym. Then I placed them back on the carpet exactly as I had found them. This small act of sabotage stretched them a little each time I found them on the floor. I slid open the large mirrored wardrobe door. It was heavy but moved smoothly to reveal Andrew's shirts. One brightly coloured designer shirt screamed at me amongst white work shirts. He would not have chosen that shirt. I shunted the other shirts along the bar. I pulled the loud shirt close and I held the top button between my fingers and twisted it round in a clockwise direction, and then in the other direction, as if opening a safe. The thin white cotton holding the button in place loosened over time, until the button remained attached only by a thin thread.

*

During this time, my wholesale sun hat business had been slowly building. I was part of a group working on a co-ordinated sun-protection campaign negotiating with school districts, hospitals, medical insurers and health researchers.

We were on the cusp of making change, of introducing hats into all school districts, but this vision was taking time to implement. If my business took off, not only would American children benefit, I could be financially independent in the US and choose to stay or leave. Through my interactions with Californian schools, I had discovered that while schools wanted to sell hats as a fun item to raise money for schools, the majority didn't want children wearing hats for sun protection, even schools with school uniforms, like my children's school. Ironically, mothers were proving to be the impediment to children wearing hats at school. They didn't want their daughters to have 'hat hair', or they thought the broad brim on the hats prevented their children from playing basketball.

I ran out of time to convince these mothers to choose hats to protect their children. I had to let go of my dream for financial independence in America. I had to do everything I could to make money quickly and that meant converting the warehouse of hats into cash. There was a madness we lived with and each day required a new plan for survival and escape. I took the hats down to the pier at Long Beach where I had seen men fishing and I individually approached fishermen and labourers working in the sun to sell hats for some cash with which to buy food.

*

I looked down from the kitchen window to the garage area below. Andrew was standing outside the car, talking to our daughters, who remained strapped in the backseat. From this window a few months earlier, I had seen a mother helping her son pack his belongings into a van because he was going to fight in Iraq. He was our neighbour and a student at Long

Beach University. He was short, but strong, aged about eighteen. Once, he had helped me to carry my groceries from Trader Joe's in thick paper bags through the heavy metal security door of our apartment block and up the stairs.

That morning, packing their van as Andrew left for work, I'd heard his mother apologise for blocking our garage area.

'He only joined the army to get an education – we couldn't afford it otherwise,' she had sobbed.

I turned away from the window that day. I didn't want to see a mother packing for her son to fight in a war against other mother's sons, a son who couldn't afford an education, a son who wasn't even old enough to legally drink a beer.

*

The events leading up to this day had involved enlisting trusted friends into my escape plan. I smuggled our passports to our neighbour. Individual items of sentimental value were trafficked to trusted friends' houses for safekeeping. These friends had been incredibly supportive throughout my time in America. What I hadn't expected in that situation was the number of strangers who also helped. Like an underground movement, these women were even prepared to break rules in their jobs to help. These women didn't doubt a word of my story, because I found out it was also their story. The Bank of America teller who helped me secure money from the joint bank account which required both signatures, had been in the same situation. The removalist company employee, who said she would switch the delivery address for our possessions to return to my mum's address in Australia rather than wherever Andrew had sent them, did so because she, too, had been in my situation. Still, this was a conversation over the phone after the goods had been packed and addressed, so I couldn't be sure if this would happen or not. I assumed she had taken a risk in her job to try to make this happen. So many women I came across had been in my situation that when I read it, I was not surprised by the finding in the *State of the World's Fathers* report that approximately one in three women globally experience violence at the hands of a male partner. In Australia, half of the women experiencing violence at the hands of a male partner or former partner have children.

*

One day, when we were living separated, I went with classmates from my writing group to attend the *LA Times* Festival of Books. We returned home just in time for school pick up. My friends realised I was in trouble when my car wasn't in the garage and they could hear me becoming more desperate on the phone with Andrew, who refused to tell me where he'd parked it. My friends drove me to collect the children, and then helped me look for the car.

The next week, those same friends from my writing group invited my daughters and I to see our first ice hockey game. They bought Sonia and Olivia Long Beach Ice Dogs beanies to wear. A couple of months later they invited me for a meal. During dinner, they slid an envelope across the table. They placed their hands over my hands.

'Spend this money in whatever way you see fit.'

'*This is not a loan*' was written on the outside of the envelope. Inside the envelope was enough cash to fly the three of us back to Australia.

Bound

*

I looked back out the kitchen window to see what was happening in the car downstairs. Andrew was still there, so I looked away. I wanted to respect their privacy and their time together, but then, when I looked down at the car again, I noticed Andrew was sitting in the driver's seat, when he was meant to be saying goodbye to the girls in the back seat. I feared he was preparing to drive off with our daughters. I bolted down the stairs, skimming two or three at a time. My breath was short when I got to the bottom. I saw he hadn't driven off, but he had taken something from the front seat and had it under his arm. He pushed past me as I reached the car. I couldn't see what he was holding. The girls were still in their seatbelts in the backseat, silent. I looked around. My laptop bag was missing.

My laptop had the family photographs, the sun hat business documents, and the work I had written for the writing group on its hard drive with no back up. I stood up to give chase. Then I stopped. I returned to the car. I checked on the girls. I drove away.

BRAIDING

The Return

As our flight neared Sydney, I felt a strange weightlessness. It wasn't emptiness or lightness. I wasn't exhausted or excited, I wasn't scared and I wasn't thrilled. None of us had slept, but Sonia and Olivia were in good spirits, possibly because we had just eaten the miniature Magnum ice creams served at three am. The girls were colouring in small books with the pencils provided in their Qantas Adventure Kit. I wasn't really viewing this new stage of our lives as an adventure.

Picking up on their light mood, I leaned across to Olivia and flippantly said, 'In Australia, you'll have to call me mummy, instead of mommy.'

Olivia, who had no recollection of calling me anything other than mommy, was horrified.

'Aren't you going to be my mommy anymore?'

I quickly explained the difference between Australian English and American English, and backtracked, saying that I would always be her mommy and her mummy. Then I remembered the die poking into me from my jeans pocket, which I had picked up from the carpet under the door of her old bedroom, and I gave it to her. She took it, but the look on her face made it clear that I had just added to her confusion. I hoped she didn't see the die as a sign of uncertainty about our future.

Her reaction made me realise that my identity was in fact confusing. I was both mummy and mommy, I was still married, but I was a single mother, I had no job and no income, at the same time as I was a business owner that operated globally. I might or might not have belongings; we had to wait six weeks to find out. I was a homeowner with a mortgage and yet I had nowhere to live.

Perhaps it was the confusion that led Olivia to quietly inform me she was about to throw up. I quickly located the plane's paper bag from the seat pocket in front, which she filled. Then she vomited in my paper bag that I had provided to her as a back-up. Olivia's vomit made Sonia feel sick, so she threw up, too. I began to feel nauseous as well, but all three sick bags had been used and the flight attendants were strapped in their seats. I dipped my head to control the waves of nausea stirring through me. I had no choice but to yell, 'Sick bag!' in the hope that someone in one of the nearby seats would offer theirs. I took my hand away from my mouth and repeated, 'Sick bag!' Nothing came. I searched my handbag for a suitable receptacle. Bending down to look just made the nausea feel more urgent. Next to my bag on the floor was the zipped Qantas Adventure Kit pencil case. I snatched it, spilled the pencils and playing cards onto the carpet below my seat and immediately barfed into it.

At the airport, my friend Linda, who had visited us the year before in Long Beach, greeted us as we arrived and was astonished at how much we had all changed. Both girls had grown taller, of course, and had bobbed haircuts. Sonia had grown new large teeth and Olivia had expanded her vocabulary, having been quiet and shy for the first three years. The girls ran to greet her. But what Linda was mostly focused on was how skinny I'd become.

*

In the background our genogram would have changed, too. A perpendicular line cut across the horizontal line binding my circle to Andrew's square to indicate a separation. Soon it would be cut again by another perpendicular line to show a broken marriage, but the original line binding Andrew and me would remain, even in divorce. I would still be drawn as the circle connected to the square, like a balloon forever tied down by a heavy block. Although genograms are meant to represent family dynamics, they don't allow for movement. The first square and the circle to the left of it stay in that same position, whether people separate, divorce, die or connect with new circles or squares. Genograms represent husband and wife as an unmovable base; they are taken to be the norm and any changes to this are represented as diversions from this norm. The date of the divorce would join the date of the marriage above the line.

*

Linda drove us to my mum's house. I was so grateful to her for letting us stay, but I wasn't so comfortable with being dependent on my mother when I was myself a mother. Nothing was said, in fact, the separation was never even mentioned, but I soon sensed her dissatisfaction with the living arrangement, too. My mother and I interacted as if the girls and I had just returned from holidays and were about to resume a normal suburban life.

Until I could sort things out, I was to sleep in my old bedroom and the children were to sleep on Mum's lounge room floor. They were excited to be 'camping at Nanny's house'. I loved how they saw the fun in all situations. They seemed adaptable and resilient, but as soon as I could, I took them to see a social worker. Thankfully, this social worker didn't start the session by drawing our genogram. Instead, she asked Sonia and Olivia if they would like to draw their own picture of their family. She offered them large sheets of white paper and the choice of Textas or crayons. The assignment excited them and they started drawing immediately.

Olivia drew four people inside a car as stick figures with fingers, toes and hair. In her picture, a man and a woman were seated in the front of the car behind an extra-large steering wheel. Two children were seated in the back.

'We're all in the car, but no one is driving,' Olivia said when prompted by the social worker. 'And there's no brake.'

Sonia had drawn two figures, one a man and one a woman. Then she coloured over them with violent Texta strokes of yellow, orange and red.

'It's Mum and Dad on fire,' she said.

The girls had captured the mood of the house, the fights, the feeling that things were out of control. I'd never felt so ashamed or saddened. They made it clear that I had done the right thing for them by leaving, after so long when I had thought I was doing the right thing by them for trying to fix the marriage. I would give everything to make their future so much better.

*

A month later, Olivia had to start kindergarten again in another country. Friends had given me the school tunic for her to wear, but I had no money to pay for her school shoes. I presumed she could get away with wearing runners for a while, having arrived back from overseas. I had no idea when Andrew had returned to Australia, or where he was living, but he appeared at the school for Olivia's first day. Olivia took turns happily running between us from one side of the playground to the other for hugs and photographs. Then she schlepped up the large concrete stairs, dwarfed by her new school backpack. Her teacher, Mr Baddington, greeted her at the door and they disappeared behind it. She didn't look back. It was only me and some other mothers left crying in the playground on the first day of big school.

When I returned to pick her up that afternoon, Mr Baddington took the time to inform me of the day's events. Olivia had settled well and was very confident with her reading, given she'd already attended kindergarten in America. Then he told me that, out of the blue, she had said, 'My parents have splitted up!' My eyes began to well. I worried about what he was going to say next. I was relieved to hear that he had responded by saying, 'My family have splitted up, too.' Then he took her to the large glass tank at the side of the room to let her feed the fish and the axolotl. I found small kindnesses and moments of understanding and caring shown to my daughters from people so uplifting.

Elaborate Covers

Five days after arriving back in Australia, I borrowed a black and white jacket, sensible interview shoes and a bag from a friend and went for an interview for some short-term contract work. I was successful. I had to evaluate programs run by schools and preschools that helped children transition to school. I was grateful for the work, but I would only be paid a small sum up front and not be paid the rest until completion of the evaluation in three months' time. I would have to use some money to buy a laptop to complete the work, given I didn't know the whereabouts of my laptop. In the meantime, I had to compete with school students to book hourly sessions on a computer at the local library.

In that same week, when my daughters were at school and my mother was out, instead of going to the library, I decided to freely explore my childhood home. My first destination was my mother's bedroom. I turned the long metal handle and the wooden door scraped along the carpet, opening into the familiar smell of lavender grown in Mum's garden, dried and kept in drawers throughout the house.

I gently sat on the outer edge of my mother's bed, careful not to make a dent, and looked across to her dressing table topped with a scallop-edged mirror like an old-fashioned bride and groom decoration on a wedding cake. I didn't recognise myself in the reflection. The story of the last few years was recorded in the deep lines scraped into my face, particularly at the centre of the forehead – the area the yoga teacher had referred to as the seat of wisdom. I stood up to take a closer look. My seat of wisdom had collapsed in on itself. I was wearing the cropped pants I had before I left for America as I hadn't bought any new clothes, but the way these pants hung off my hips made them look like they belonged to someone else.

Sunlight pressed through the shapes of the lace curtain, then refracted off the crystal vase on the dressing table to shower the room with soft rainbows. I imagined my mother bathing in them while taking an afternoon nap on the bed with her cavoodle. This made me smile and stop looking at myself.

The heavy crystal set on the dressing table – vase, tray, perfume bottle and a round jar with a lid – had been my mother's wedding presents. These were precious objects I was never allowed to hold as a child for fear I'd drop them. On the crystal tray was a brush and hand mirror laid out like surgeon's tools, probably since the first day Mum and Dad moved into the house. That squarish-headed brush and I have long known the contours of Mum's once-rich auburn hair. When I was young, Mum and I used to watch classic Hollywood films from her black and white era together. In them, glamorous women sat at their dressing tables and prepared for bed by making themselves pleasing for their husbands.

Mum's tray rested on a delicate white doily of handmade lace, an intricacy of snowflakes patterning the edges. My mother would have sewn the doily as a teenager, under the watchful eye of her teacher who, if the detailed needlework was not precise, would have made her start again. On completion, my mother would have wrapped the doily in waxed paper, gently placed it into her wooden glory box and wished for a husband, the time at which her needlework would again see light.

While my father had his shed as his exclusive space, my mother had the dressing table. The popularity of dressing tables in my mother's era suggests that the mothers of that generation had time to sit and take care of themselves. I hope they did.

The permanent, ordered contents of the dressing table told a story of stability and genuine happily-ever-afters. My life, by contrast, was in flux. My marriage had ended. Our belongings were in transit, packed together and still to be divided. I couldn't be certain where they would end up or when they would arrive and, either way, conflict would follow.

I suppose my laptop was the equivalent of my mum's crystal vanity set. I had bought my laptop when I became a mother because that's when I started working from home and it had been the one constant in my life since. At least that's how Olivia saw it. I had become aware of this at a Mother's Day afternoon tea at her preschool when we were in America. Mrs Bailey asked the children questions about their mothers and wrote down their answers. Olivia described my hair as black, but it is brown. She described my eyes as red, but they are a blue-grey. When asked what her mother likes best, Olivia answered, 'Her computer.' She had drawn a picture of me at a desk with my computer from her perspective, so it looked as though she was excluded from the intimate relationship I had with that object. It made me more conscious to take her perspective into account.

Seeing myself again in Mum's scalloped mirror, I wondered when I had stopped taking care of myself – cleansing, toning, moisturising, flossing, wearing make-up, exercising were no longer part of a routine. Since becoming a mother, attention to myself beyond brushing my teeth had become a time waster. Even the vigorous brushing of my teeth each morning was done while simultaneously cleaning from the basin the thick trails of toothpaste left by those who had brushed their milk teeth before me.

In the bathroom of my childhood home, the combined smells of eucalyptus, Exit Mould and Glen 20 made me sneeze and brought back memories of a furry orange cover stretched over the toilet lid, somehow designed to match a crocheted purple doll that covered the toilet rolls standing alongside it. The more toilet rolls that were placed under that doll's crocheted skirt, the straighter the doll stood – which seemed a poor design, considering the purpose for which she was made.

Mum's Sunbeam Mixmaster, also a wedding present, was hidden under a bespoke floral cotton cover of reds and greens that matched the one covering the Breville Kitchen Wizz and toaster. The teapot when hot wore a striped knitted cosy. Tissues were accessed through a country-crafted wooden cover. Clothes hung off wooden coat hangers disguised as pink crocheted sausages. It occurred to me that my mum had spent a lot of time lovingly sewing, knitting, embroidering, crocheting and country-crafting elaborate covers in the effort to not have things exposed. It occurred to me, too, that when we returned to our own house where we used to live, just like the doll in the toilet, the more I could keep under my skirts, so to speak, the more upstanding I might be perceived to be.

My biggest concern, however, was not what I should tell others, but what I should tell my daughters. I wanted them to love their father, as they did, but I also needed to know they were safe. I wanted them to be empowered to know what was and wasn't respectful behaviour. I wanted them to understand what was happening and why. I wanted us to always be open with each other. I had been that toilet roll doll: I had kept it all under my skirts for years. They were only five and seven. When was the time to tell them the truth, so that they could understand and be able to handle any situation? The social work advice was, 'Don't ever say anything bad about their father. They'll only hate you for it.'

In the corner of the lounge room, I paused in front of the mantelpiece above the bricked-up fireplace. I ran my fingers along the tapestry there. I folded back a corner to see the stretch and tuck of each colourful strand of my mother's needlework; it was meticulous. I marvelled at my mum's abilities.

Above the tapestry in that silver frame, I was shocked to find myself still there as a smiling bride, as if nothing had changed. I suppose my mum was in a difficult position, not knowing what to do. I would have preferred if she had discreetly removed the photograph before I returned, so I wouldn't have had to face it or have it potentially confuse my daughters. I'm sure she hoped we would get back together. I used to believe this photograph symbolised that Andrew and I would be as solid as a rock and that he would always be there to offer support when needed. I went close to examine the younger me with a husband I had to leave, holding me suspended over a cliff; I saw then that I could have brought a different interpretation to that photograph.

*

Later that week, on the type of day my mother would have referred to as a perfect day for doing the washing, the girls and I were walking Mum's cavoodle along her street, absorbing the brilliant Australian sunlight. Olivia was walking the dog ahead of us and Sonia was holding my hand and chatting. We came upon a cluster of white frangipani flowers with yellow centres on the grass. For me, these flowers hold the fragrance of summer. We chose the most recently fallen flowers to place behind our ears. We were pretending to be Hawaiian hula dancers moving our hips. We joked about who would clean up the dog poo. At the same time, Mum's next-door neighbour, Mr Cooper, approached. His spine was curved into a question mark but he moved swiftly, aided by a stick. Mr Cooper and his wife were great friends to my mother. They often popped into Mum's house on Sundays, after their return from mass at the local Catholic Church.

'Hello, Mr Cooper,' I greeted him. 'These are my daughters, Sonia and Olivia.'

Mr Cooper made no acknowledgement. He walked right past. I thought he must not have heard me, or perhaps he hadn't recognised me as I'd lost so much weight.

'Mr Cooper,' I said louder. He stopped on the grass after he had passed and turned back to face us. He pointed at me with the hand holding his walking stick and said fervently, 'You should be ashamed of yourself!' Then he walked on.

Stunned, I didn't know what to say to my daughters. We all instinctively began running back to Mum's house. I bagged the dog poo and we legged it, the poo jiggling up and down in the bag as I ran.

Why would he say such a thing? Should we not have picked the flowers off the grass and put them in our hair? Perhaps he thought we had picked the flowers from the tree. Did he think it was wrong to dance in the street? Had he heard us joking about not wanting to pick up the dog poo and thought we wouldn't pick it up?

For some weird reason, I also wondered why someone who needed to lean on a walking stick would use the hand with their stick to point and not their free hand.

It wasn't until we entered the house and passed my wedding photo that it suddenly became clear to me.

I approached Mum, who was sitting in the sunroom, reading a gardening magazine.

'Mum, what did you say to Mr Cooper?'

'Mr Cooper... I just told him about your situation.'

'My situation?'

'Yes.'

'You don't even talk to *me* about *my situation*.' Not only did I emphasise the words, I used hand gestures to show quotation marks around 'my situation'.

'If you're staying in my house, the neighbours need to know.'

'What do they need to know? Mum, this is my private life!'

'You told me to tell everyone before you returned from America.'

'I meant the family, not the neighbours. I wanted you to tell the family, so I wouldn't have to answer all their stupid, hurtful questions when I returned. I couldn't face that. I didn't mean for you to tell everyone in the street!'

'Calm down.'

I knew I needed to calm down. I wanted to calm down. I wanted to calm Mum down, but I couldn't. I was shaking and she was shaking, but I couldn't calm down.

I lifted my wedding photo off the mantelpiece.

'If you've told everyone about my situation, why is this still here?'

'You were the one who wanted me to display it.'

'You don't understand anything.' Even as I said this, and stormed off, I reminded myself that I had not actually told Mum anything.

Snow Dome

I expected that ending the marriage would end the violence. I was wrong. As it turns out, separation can be the time of greatest danger for a woman. In Australia, one woman a week is murdered by her current or former partner.

I was at his apartment, where I was to collect the children after their weekend with him as we'd agreed. He refused to give them back. When he started pushing me backwards, two flights of stairs lay behind me. The Parenting Orders were still being tossed in a game between our lawyers. The Family Court process gave no clear rules in situations where couples did not agree. It was a situation that allowed for bullying. On that Sunday afternoon, the children were inside his apartment, looking out through the open door. They didn't move or make a sound when I arrived. He came out of his apartment, shut the door and started to push me towards the steps. His neighbour heard me scream. She came out after Andrew had returned to his apartment and she invited me into her apartment. She gave me water and let me rest. This was the first time he had done something so public. Instead of me just returning home to deal with it on my own, that brave neighbour reinforced that what had just happened was real and that it was not reasonable behaviour. She encouraged me to call the police from her phone. I called and, at the insistence of the officer I spoke to, we started the process of going to court for an Apprehended Domestic Violence Order.

*

On the morning of the court appearance, it looked like beer o'clock in a city pub on a Friday afternoon. Suits, noise, movement. But it wasn't. It was nine o'clock in a suburban courthouse. A crisp April morning. So many men in suits. Bloke-ing around, shaking hands, patting backs. Solicitors, prosecutors, perpetrators. I couldn't tell the difference. They were lit by the sun shining through a large, round skylight. Some suits were broader than the shoulders under them; others were worn like a second skin. Andrew looked comfortable enough in his, talking to his lawyer: 'I can't believe it... there's no grounds... mental health problems.' I felt the muscles in my body tighten, snapping back into familiar places.

I moved to where a police officer sat locked inside a glass booth like a ticket seller for an exclusive show. Without eye contact, she repeated my name, louder than I would have liked, and turned to the second page of her list. She ticked my name and then pointed with her pen to the purpose-built room behind her. Another police officer, solid and focused on the men pacing outside, punched a code that opened its double-glazed door. No one looked up as I entered. The door closed automatically behind me and my ears found it hard to adjust to the instant silence.

A different police officer checked the details of my case in the police report and she asked me to take a seat inside this glassed-in room with the other women that were there. On a wooden bench that ran along the wall sat women of all ages and walks of life. Most were alone. Some of the younger women had their mothers with them, or a female friend. I didn't see any brothers, fathers or male friends. I wondered, if some men had come to support their sisters, daughters or friends, whether they would be allowed inside with the women or be asked to sit outside with the other men.

At the centre of the room, a truck without wheels, some wooden blocks and hardcover children's books littered the floor. One of the books I recognised: *Guess How Much I Love You?* Toddlers quietly held toys as babies quietly held their mothers, mothers quietly held cardboard cups filled with coffee. We could have been mistaken for a very dull playgroup. I was glad my children were at school.

No politician could claim to be ignorant of the impacts of domestic violence on children – witnessing or hearing it – they were listed in a submission to the Australian Parliament in 2011. These impacts include depression, anxiety, increased aggression, antisocial behaviour, low self-esteem, pervasive fear, impaired thinking and an increased likelihood of drug or alcohol abuse. Even the health of family pets has been shown to suffer in houses where there is abuse.

Looking out of the glass walls, it made me feel like I was inside a large snow dome composed of local families that had been vigorously shaken: the women and children motionless figures set in the middle; the men swirling around the outside; all contained within a glass-domed building. It was like a microcosm of normative family life: children at the centre, women in an inner dome, men outside. No reporters or law students were allowed in the courthouse on these days: Domestic Violence Tuesday and Domestic Violence Thursday. Twice a week, every week, except Christmas Day.

I scanned the room. Some women were wearing suits and some were wearing bruises. Some clearly wore what they'd had on when they fled the house. I was wearing a suit; I'd deliberately powered up to feel confident and to be taken seriously. I wanted my day in court. I wanted the violence to stop. Then, when a woman in baggy track pants and a dirty T-shirt moved along the bench to create a space for me, I felt conscious about how I was dressed. I could feel her bony hip at the top of her leg, which jerked up and down from the ball of her foot like a jackhammer. Her movement took my focus, the speed of it: up-down-up-down-up-down. I wanted to offer her solace, to help her calm down, but I was getting drawn into her nervous rhythm, up-down-up-down-up-down, and I couldn't afford to do that. I breathed out long, slow, audible sighs and didn't make eye contact, and I didn't look at the children on the floor, and I didn't look at the women with bruises, and I resisted that rhythm, and I took hold of my feelings and I squeezed them all back inside my suit.

'Hastings, Azapardi, Tran,' a police officer called. They silently left our circle through the heavily glazed door, as a fresh-looking social worker and some older women entered. These were the amazing women of the Women's Domestic Violence Court Advocacy Service, offering invaluable support to the women through the court process. The young social worker was not there for that role. I knew she was a social worker because she held a thick blue diary, like the one I used to carry. These diaries contained a wealth of information – weights and measures conversion tables, international paper sizes and world standard times – but no prompts to help solve complex social problems. The social worker was talking with each woman. She spoke in a high voice with a positive tone and was the only person speaking. She looked and sounded familiar. Then I realised I had known her professionally. I hoped that she didn't recognise me. I looked at the floor and felt my chest rise and fall and wished for my name to be called, but not too loudly.

None of my social work roles had specifically focused on domestic violence. In reality, though, most social work roles intersect with the consequences of it. I had supported women in this situation a number of times. I had driven women and their children to shelters. In the silence of the car, I'd felt the palpable rhythm of the little heartbeats and the big heartbeat, like the *doof, doof* vibration from a rev head's subwoofer. I drove quickly, knowing that one woman is killed every week by a current or former partner, but not knowing, as I navigated traffic, if that partner or former partner was following us with his gun or his knife or his extended family. Controlled emotional involvement – that's what we were taught. To keep a distance, to not get caught up in the emotion of people's lives, to retain objectivity, wielding our thick blue diaries like a shield against overpowering emotions. Back then, I would have reassured these women by saying that it could have happened to anyone. I believed what I said, but I didn't think for a minute that that 'anyone' might include me. I had become an educated, middle-class professional. My husband was an educated, middle-class professional. He was well read, articulate, he played with his children and helped them with their homework and he vacuumed. Social workers were meant to be skilled at assessing personality, even personality disorders, and it was this oversight that was hard for me to accept. I spent way too long trying to understand how I had got it so wrong.

Snow Dome

*

Growing up, I would have said that I'd never heard of domestic violence. But that wouldn't be completely true. The semi-detached brick house where I grew up shared a wall with the neighbours. Sometimes I'd hear yelling and screaming coming from next door. Then there'd be a thud against the common wall. I remember this because my sister and I had our delicate figurines in a shadow box on our side of the wall. My grandfather made the shadow box to hold and display these trinkets – the sort of gifts that girls gave to each other for birthdays or Christmas. In the largest wooden box was a family of glass deer. We had watched a glass blower create them. With a breath, the glass blower magically pulled out transparent creatures from a bubble, using only a flame and a steady hand. I thought it magical. The thud from next door once forced these harmless animals to the wooden floor and a leg was broken. Because my sister and I were so upset, my father quickly glued the deer back together, but the reason for the yelling and screaming and the thud was never explained. So, from a young age I had heard domestic violence; I just hadn't heard its name.

*

'Fardoulis, Flint, Slattery.' Three women stood and vacated their seats. There was shuffling along the bench. The social worker moved closer. I wished for my name to be called. I kept my eyes down, so she wouldn't recognise me, and kept breathing deeply, in and out, in and out. The social worker made a little space for her tailored-trousered bottom on the bench not far from me. I overheard her explaining her purpose. She had a draft version of a pamphlet that outlined the Cycle of Violence and she wanted 'feedback' from the women in the room about the appropriateness of the colours, the pictures and the language. This was the right audience for gathering feedback, but what she hadn't realised was that this was not the right time to be gathering feedback. I was once like her, compassionate, informed and well intentioned, but without the life experience to really know what would be most helpful to these women.

*

Andrew and I sat separately at our children's performances and school presentation nights, and we stayed on opposite sides of the football field during their games.

People often said, 'Can't you just get on together for the sake of the kids?'

I wanted to respond by saying, 'Would you want to sit next to the man who smashed your head into a brick wall and then pretended it never happened?'

Instead, I said nothing. People preferred that I said nothing. A common response to my story, if I shared it – and I rarely did – was disbelief. Some friends and family were immobilised by the story I told, like cartoon characters sprayed with a giant glue gun. I needed their help, but once the facts of the matter were said, nothing was ever said again. It added to the feeling of isolation and lack of support. I did understand because I knew how easy it was to be charmed by him. On the other hand, there were friends who did help immeasurably, both in America and when we returned to Australia and they helped to change the course of our lives.

Snow Dome

*

Domestic violence and intimate partner violence were terms often used. The words 'partner', 'intimate' and 'domestic' implied complicity, something agreed upon between two people. The euphemisms were endless. These words didn't pack the punch that led to immediate action the way words like 'terrorism' or 'king hit' did. How could anyone know that the police word 'domestics' meant the biggest crime story in Australia? Police respond to an incident every two minutes. Ten women a day are hospitalised for assault injuries perpetrated by a spouse or partner. More female deaths and illness than caused by smoking or obesity or illicit drugs or alcohol or terrorism. The leading cause of preventable death, illness and disability for women aged fifteen to forty-four. This is not seen as a national health priority, like diabetes or heart disease. How would anyone know that the term 'family and domestic violence' is the leading cause of homelessness for women and children? And one in four of Australia's homeless are children. How could anyone know that intimate partner violence costs economies more in financial terms than a civil war might? The softness of the words, 'intimate partner violence', does not say that falling in love with a man could be the riskiest thing a woman could possibly do and that having a child would only increase her risk of harm from the man she loves.

*

The skylight in the ceiling of the courthouse was, I hoped, for the purpose of a benevolent force to keep an eye on things. This benevolent force might occasionally shake the snow dome, clearing the debris to reveal the dignity of its central figures. But I didn't understand why this benevolent force wouldn't rearrange things so that the women and children were on the outside. The children freed to dance and swirl as glittery flakes of snow, the women able to move about and talk, and those men locked in the central glass room, for silent reflection.

I expected to enter the courtroom when my name was called, but I found myself sitting in a smaller room with no windows and four male suits pressing in on me, urging me to drop the case. They wanted me to settle for a lesser order, a temporary protection order, rather than an Apprehended Domestic Violence Order.

'The courtroom will not be a pleasant experience,' they said.

'He may lose his job because of this,' they said. 'Then he won't be able to financially support your children.'

I wanted to say that he had never financially supported the children and he wasn't doing that now, but I remained silent.

'The magistrate will think you're making it up to get a better deal in the Family Court,' they said. The lawyer handling my divorce had advised me not to go to the police about the violence for the same reason. I couldn't believe a lawyer would discourage a woman from asking a court for protection. What my lawyer hadn't explained to me was that the Family Law Amendment (Shared Parental Responsibility) Act 2006 led to a situation where shared parenting was favoured, over protecting women and children from physical and psychological harm, because of a 'friendly parent' provision. The court worked on the assumption that children were something like belongings, to be equally shared, regardless of the relationships or care that had been provided up to that point. If a woman went to court asking for protection for herself and her children, she was seen as an 'unfriendly parent', not playing by the Family Court's rules, and was likely to get less time with her children, or in some cases none at all. Rosie Batty AO identified this as an important factor in the Family Court decisions about access and care for her son, Luke. Rosie had been seen as a 'hostile parent' and therefore her concerns for her son's safety were not believed. Despite a history of significant violence, the father was given access to his son, who he murdered with a cricket bat.

*

The suits pressured me until I agreed to apply only for a temporary protection order. I'd get temporary protection without having to fight his lawyer in court. I may have been clothed in a suit, but my undergarments were humiliation and exhaustion.

I left the court with a temporary protection order and a police frisk, only to bump into Andrew when I stepped outside. He was pale and livid.

My Situation

The sounds of freedom and friendship – skipping, bouncing, calling, running and laughter – reverberated between the classrooms as I walked across the asphalt of the school playground before the morning bell. Trying to find my daughters in the mix of children all dressed the same, from sun hat to school shoes, was impossible. I wanted to spot them so that I could avoid them seeing me. It wasn't what I usually did, but mine was another humiliating errand and I didn't want them to know about it.

'Hi, Olivia's mother. Can Olivia come to my house this afternoon?'

One of Olivia's friends walked alongside me as we weaved through children's interactions and ducked to avoid being hit by stray balls large and small.

'I suppose so, if Olivia wants to,' I replied and she skipped off happily.

Inside the silent school office, there were three possible windows for a parent or child to approach. No one looked up from any of them. The tops of three heads of the school's administration officers, two with straight hair, one with curly, was all that could be seen. I stood between all three and said to no one in particular, 'I have an appointment with the principal.'

'Purpose of the appointment?' came a voice from the window where the curly hair could be seen.

I didn't think it was any of her business, but I answered obediently.

'School fees.'

Then I saw all three faces.

'Oh!'

Mr Brewster, whose door had been opened, immediately appeared in the doorway – brown hair, brown pants, white shirt, brown cardigan. As the principal of a public primary school, Mr Brewster was known only for balancing the books. He had requested this interview; well, not directly, but he had written the following in the school newsletter:

Any family who cannot pay the voluntary school fees due to extreme financial hardship should arrange a meeting with myself without further ado to confidentially explain the circumstances as to why the voluntary fees could not be afforded to the school at this particular point in time.

When I first received the voluntary school fees statement for $145 for each daughter, I requested the administrative staff send the statement to their father, as he was their only parent who had been in permanent employment. The response from the front office was, 'Fees statements are always sent to the mother of the child.'

Mr Brewster sat on a comfortable office chair at his desk and I was offered a low, vinyl seat. The principal sat behind his desk, looking down at me.

I was there to ask one simple question, could the school please send the invoice to their father.

'School fees are always sent to the mother of the child.'

Then came a barrage of questions I didn't think were relevant to the paying of school fees.

'Are you divorced?', 'How long have you been separated?', 'Where are you living?', 'Where is their father living?'

Like a diligent child, I answered all his questions. He seemed to have no idea how private this information was, how raw my feelings were, how tactful and caring I would have preferred him to be. He didn't ask about the welfare of my daughters, who were under his duty of care. He didn't tell me how the school could support children who had just moved countries or how they'd supported other children of separated parents. He didn't offer the school's counsellor. I'd expected that the school might have processes in place, given that one in five children in Australia live in a single-parent household. I hated to think that one-fifth of the children at his school, children who had been through such conflict, family loss and dislocation, were offered no support by the school during this time.

'I'll need to see the Family Court orders.'

He was so perfunctory; he could have been asking for the minutes from a meeting. He lacked the sensitivity the moment required and appeared instead to revel in the possibilities of more paperwork.

'We don't have court orders yet,' I told him.

He persevered with questions until he pulled hot tears of humiliation out of me. Reluctantly, he shared some of his Department of Education tissues, the ones that feel like they've been recycled from the cardboard the kindergarten class use for craft. He stopped his questions after this.

'You'll need to write everything you just said in an email in order to waive the fees.'

It felt like being made to write lines as punishment.

'This will be treated in the strictest confidence,' he said, and escorted me out the door.

I typed the information I had already disclosed to him in his office and sent the email. I never received a reply. Afterwards, Sonia was denied her maths textbook, because her 'voluntary' fees were not paid. She was singled out in front of her classmates to receive a particular school envelope, which all children would have recognised as a fees envelope. I paid the fees as soon as I was paid from my first job.

*

Ending a disrespectful relationship with one person forced me to enter into many relationships with institutions that I also found to sometimes be disrespectful. The Family Court, the Child Support Agency and Centrelink all required the private details of our lives, over and over again. My children's friends' parents wanted answers, too.

'Who wanted to end it?' and, 'Does he have a girlfriend?'

Questions such as these were asked while I waited to buy chicken wings from the deli section in Coles, or at a school event during Education Week, often with my children present.

I found solace in the honesty of being a divorced single parent, compared with the time spent pretending to be part of a happily married couple. Honesty came from others, too, as I became something of a bad-weather friend. Without soliciting it, I found both mothers and fathers in the school community sought me out to share the minutiae of limping marriages or recent break-ups they felt they couldn't share with anyone else. Because I was appreciative of the people who had been there for me, I was honoured if I could be that trusted person for someone else.

On the other hand, invitations for dinner parties, tennis or weekends away with the happily married clique in the school community were rare. Such invitations were sometimes delivered when a couple had a single friend of the opposite gender who would inevitably be seated next to me, or opposite me, and his awkwardness suggested that he, too, had not been expecting such an arrangement and was similarly not receptive to the idea. At these dinners, a woman from one of the couples around the table would pat my arm as if I was ill and say such things as, 'I know just what it's like to be a single parent when my husband's away in Dubai or China for business.'

Then there was the curt invitation from a father at the school I'd never met before but who appeared in my face at the end of the school fundraiser: 'I hear you're single and I'm single, so we should get together.'

*

Each time I'd asked Sonia's teacher how Sonia was going at school, she'd preface her answer with the statement, 'Knowing about your situation...', but I had not informed her of 'my situation', and had no idea what she understood to be 'my situation'. I began to doubt my 'confidential chat' with the principal had been confidential at all.

Despite her teacher seemingly knowing about 'my situation', there was no understanding shown to Sonia if she left her homework, her school jumper or hat at her father's house and couldn't get it until he returned from work that night. Sonia, along with other children who had possibly left school items at one of their parents' houses, were made to stand in front of the assembly.

The irony of my daughter being singled out at school for not having a sun hat when I had left these same hats in a warehouse in the United States, because their schools did not want to use them, was not lost on me. Sonia's school could simply have provided a locker, a cupboard or a box under desks where children could leave their hat, library bag, sports shoes, spare jumper or clarinet, for the many children who live in two homes during the week. Instead, a child needed to remember all the items required each time they moved between houses.

I rang the school anonymously to complain about the practice of singling children out to stand at the front of the assembly and they did stop doing it. The damage had already been done, however, as Sonia began to worry each morning that something would go wrong. She worried she'd forgotten something and would be singled out. She loved learning, but started to dread going to school. She began to cry sometimes before school and sometimes at school. She instructed me to stay in the playground until the end of assembly and stay in her sight until she entered the classroom. This way she could get through the day. She also needed me to be standing in the doorway when the children spilled out of the classroom in the afternoon. I wasn't going to let her down and she needed to see that. Her teacher was not so enthusiastic about this strategy.

When this was happening, I wouldn't reach work until after ten, and I had to leave at two-thirty to be the first face she saw when the bell rang. I had therefore only taken a short-term, part-time project job at an hourly rate I hadn't had since graduating fifteen years earlier, but it was close to home and flexible, so I was able to spread the hours I worked over the week to be there when Sonia needed me.

As I dressed for work one morning, Sonia entered my bedroom dressed for school. She walked across the room with her shoulders heavy and slumped across my bed, belly down, as if her ordinarily muscular body had lost its backbone.

'I don't think I can get through the day, she said.

This was unprecedented. Sonia had never feared anything. In kindergarten, when she had started wearing glasses and I had feared she might be picked on, as kids had done at my school to children who wore glasses, Sonia had just laughed and said she was lucky to have four eyes instead of two. Now her indomitable spirit had given way to an insidious fear of all the things that could go wrong, and it overpowered her. At eight years old, instead of excitedly leaving early for school, as she used to, there was so much going on in her life, that the daily ritual of school had already proven too much. It saddened me to see her so debilitated.

I thought that with the right support she could build coping skills to help her to get through each day. Even though I had more knowledge of services than most parents, there was no service for her. The social worker with whom Sonia had built a relationship when we returned from overseas could only be involved at the initial stage of separation. The counselling services she needed were provided for teenagers, but not for eight-year-olds. I didn't consider the school counsellor who came to the school twice a week would be that helpful, given the uncaring attitude I'd received from the principal and the lack of confidentiality. There were excellent group programs I knew of, but they were only run once or twice a year. There was a three-month wait before the next one. All services required the written consent of both parents, but

Andrew denied there was a problem when she was with him, insisting that I must be making her this way.

I tried elements of psychological strategies – positive self-talk, de-catastrophising, cognitive behaviour therapy. I showed Sonia the cartoon-like drawings inside Seligman's book, *The Optimistic Child*. Then I tried interventions that I had only just started to learn – meditation, breathing, visualisation, affirmations. Then came dream catchers, pink bubbles of protection, carrying empowering objects and adopting fearless animals as symbols – sometimes all at the same time. Each morning, I offered one approach after the next in an effort to assist her to contain the emotions that wanted to spill out. She used all her strength to hold those emotions in for the school day. Some of her friends at school understood and helped her, and some of the other mothers saw her struggling in the playground and sat with her. I was so grateful for the wonderful community of friends and neighbours that offered support. I found out years later that other children had suffered in the same way at this time and those parents were also at a loss to know how to help or how to get help.

I was emotionally drained each day when I arrived at work. Colleagues who were also single parents had seen it all before. They reassured me that we were going through the hardest part, and that things would get better. I found this reassuring. I said similar things to Sonia. I hoped it was true, but I had no way of knowing.

Pirates

Within months of arriving back in Sydney, once I had a regular job, we returned to our family home. I'd had to take over full responsibility for the mortgage repayments, as Andrew refused to pay anything, not knowing if I'd be able to keep the house in the settlement. Friends and family arrived with cake, teapots, farm-fresh eggs and flowers in a vase. They lent us pans for cooking, chairs for sitting and mattresses for sleeping. My sister supplied us with her daughter's clothes as soon as she grew out of them. Linda and Georgette were regular visitors on weekends until Georgette was too frail and we became regular visitors at her house. Linda made a regular game of bath time as she soaped the girls' hair into knotty crowns of suds. As I took on more work, Mum helped by picking up Sonia and Olivia from school two afternoons a week and making dinner on those nights. My neighbours, Carol and Phil, sent their sons to mow our lawn and later, when they saw me painting the bathroom one night, they brought their portable speaker across, picked up a brush and joined in. On other afternoons when I worked, mothers from the school offered my daughters play dates with their children after school until I came to pick them up. It was the first time I understood the true value of family, friends and community.

When my sister came to visit and saw that we had no furniture, she offered to drive me around her suburb of houses known as McMansions during Council Clean Up Week. My sister and I had always had fun sharing a bedroom when we lived together. I don't remember any fighting or jealousy. She was five years older, so when I was still at school, and she was working, she'd kindly take me out for pizza and movies and let me wear her fancy work clothes any time I wanted. She'd drive me from Punchbowl to Cronulla beach with the radio blaring and all the windows down, our long blonde hair blowing across our faces wearing only our bikinis. But we had drifted apart over the years. We lost the closeness we had formed through twenty years of sharing a bedroom. I suppose it was not appropriate that my sister should be seen on the street picking at her neighbours' rubbish, but she had the heart to offer to do this with me as a way to help me out.

*

My first professional role was as a community development worker on a public housing estate in south western Sydney. I got to know the families that lived there very well. Inside their homes, I drank dark, rich coffee and ate homemade sponge cakes and moon cakes and baklava as I listened to their stories. Their stories followed a familiar arc: life was kicking along well enough and then something happened – they lost their job, or their health, or someone they loved lost their health and they became their carer, or they had to flee their country to save their life, or flee their house to save their life, and so on. This sounded like bad luck, to me. Luck, however, is not a social work theory.

The job description was 'to work with the residents to meet their needs'. 'Needs' was meant at a community level, not an individual level. I had been taught strategies for this, but there was a constant stream of people through the door with an immediate personal need for nappies or baby formula or furniture that they couldn't afford to buy. I had the unusual power to grant people free access to second-hand furniture supplied by charities. It wasn't at all a prime aspect of the role, but if someone was destitute, they could approach me and, with my signature on the organisation's letterhead and a summary of their financial circumstances, they could be given a second-hand wardrobe from a charity, instead of paying for it. Although I saw myself as a helping professional, to that person I was just another bureaucrat they had to tell their sad story to in order to get a lousy wardrobe that someone had thrown out. Charity shops are always full of goods people have donated, while people remain in need, and I have never understood that. I was bypassing that process but for some reason, even when people had thrown their rubbish on the street, to take it felt like stealing.

I remembered one such charity telling me that most of their clients were single parents, but their advertisements asking for financial donations couldn't reflect that because they believed their donors would not see a lone mother and her family as deserving. One advertisement showed a family with a mum and dad, where Dad had lost his job. Another focused on a blue-eyed girl with scuffed shoes and a hand-me-down uniform sitting alone in the school playground. She didn't come with a backstory.

*

Our suburban furniture adventure didn't begin well. There was an awkward silence in the car as we slid through mute cul-de-sacs in my sister's Toyota Kluger, feeling eyes penetrating from behind recently dusted plantation shutters. If she slowed the car, dogs barked to protect their family's knoll of discarded goods. Neither my sister nor I had whatever was needed to propel us out of the car to fossick through piles of other people's junk.

Then I remembered the large envelopes that had been arriving in my letterbox. They featured the distinct kangaroo and emu coat of arms of the federal government. In the past, such a letter would herald an opportunity – an invitation to vote or a passport. Recently, such letters were from the Family Court, Child Support Agency or Centrelink. Letters from the Child Support Agency were the easiest to spot: never folded, even if the letter could easily fit into a smaller envelope. I didn't know how they would fit into a standard letterbox, mine was generously made for me by my uncle who knew I had professional journals delivered and so had made it exceptionally large.

When I arrived back in Australia with no partner, no money, no savings, no job and few possessions, I applied for jobs. I also contacted Centrelink, believing they were the agency that assisted families if they found themselves temporarily in a situation without money.

'You have to apply to request money from the father before Centrelink can assess you for financial support,' was the response. I'd spent the last two years trying to do that. I have no idea why there is a public perception that all single mothers receive payments from Centrelink, but that is definitely not the case.

I had to approach the Child Support Agency to ask Andrew to contribute financially to support his children. The Child Support Agency is a misnomer. It does not offer support. It merely collects money from separated or divorced parents and redistributes it between them. The aim is noble, that parents share in the cost of supporting their children according to their capacity. As always, the devil is in the detail. I know that this would be a difficult task to administer and I have spoken to enough mothers and fathers to know that everyone feels wronged by the system, but there are also many ways it could be improved. It is a faceless organisation. When I called the helpline, I was sent *The Parent's Guide to Child Support*, outlining the system I had to join. On page 15 of this booklet, their formulas were outlined in a way they thought every traumatized parent going through a separation would understand:

> *We add both parents' child support incomes together to get a combined child support income. We divide each parent's individual child support income by the combined child support income to get an income percentage. We work out each parent's care percentage of the child. We work out the cost percentage of the child. We subtract the cost percentage from the income percentage for each parent. The result is called the child support percentage. If it's a negative percentage, that parent may receive child support because their share of the costs of raising the children is more than met by the amount of care they are providing. If it's a positive percentage, that parent needs to pay child support because they aren't meeting the costs of the child directly through care... We get the final child support payable by multiplying the positive child support percentage by the costs of the child.*

A brief letter that arrived from the Child Support Agency in a large envelope listed our case number, one page of calculations and the total amount to be paid by said parent for the financial support of his children. The total was $0.00. I thought it was a typo. It wasn't.

In the year Andrew had returned to his permanent job in Australia, after working for the past two years in the United States (while I gave up my job and had no job to return to), the amount he had to contribute towards the cost of raising his children was zero.

I was told to approach Legal Aid for advice in relation to Child Support. There was a Legal Aid centre that serviced the area where I lived, but they couldn't advise me because Andrew was their client and to assist me would be a conflict of interest. I thought Andrew's income would have disqualified him for Legal Aid, and my lack of income would have qualified me. I couldn't go to a different Legal Aid as they only serviced people in their local area.

It took hours of phone conversations with the Child Support Agency only to discover that the Child Support Agency determines rates based on the Australian Tax Office's income assessment for the previous tax year. Because Andrew had earned American dollars, he didn't have to file a tax return in Australia, so his taxable income in Australia was considered to be $0.00 for child support purposes. The money he was earning in Australia would determine the Child Support Agency payment after he completed his next year's tax return. The system expected that my children and I could just disappear for another year, or whenever Andrew decided to file a tax return.

I was used to advocating for others who were vulnerable and unable to advocate for themselves; there was dignity in that. I saw no dignity in advocating for my children's father to pay towards the cost of raising them. I had to apply in writing for an appeal. The process took months. When Andrew was deemed eligible to contribute towards the costs of raising his children, he refused to pay. The Child Support Agency did nothing. I had to follow them up. They informed me that they could deduct the child support payment from his pay, but I had to request this in writing. His employer, the New South Wales government, took a further three months to set this up. It shocked me that this happened to mothers and children in Australia, with seemingly no concern as to how they are living with no income in the meantime. I was not the only mother in this situation. Almost a quarter of fathers who are assessed as needing to pay child support have not done so. The Child Support Agency itself reported that in 2019, the amount owed by fathers to mothers in their system was $1.6 billion. Politicians were concerned about the national debt and government chased individual Centrelink clients if there was perceived to be any debt owed, but I had never heard a politician mention this debt, I had never heard of the government putting resources into recovering this debt. Instead, I could see how this situation forced women with their children who had left abusive situations into poverty, and allowed for the partners they had left to continue their financial abuse.

For me, this happened during Australia's golden era of wealth, when the prime minister liked to repeatedly inform me that the mining boom had allowed me to be better off financially than any other Australian before me. It was odd to have slid so easily from being in a revered position, having an education and a career, being married, being a parent, to feeling so invisible and abandoned by my own society. I left a marriage where I had been made to feel worthless. To then be treated like this, brought out in me a feeling I had not felt before. Rage.

The Child Support Agency gave a standard response if your tone had an air of complaint: 'If you're not happy with our service, you can opt out and have the child's father pay you directly.' This was said to parents whom they knew had left abusive relationships.

To add to the insult, the Child Support Agency included with its letter a glossy booklet that advised separated parents on how they should raise their children. The images they chose to accompany the text made life look like a perpetual five-year-old's birthday party, if you were lucky enough to be a child of separated parents. Child Support Agency children swam, cartwheeled, paddled canoes, picked flowers and wore designer clothes while being piggybacked by handsome dads. These booklets reminded me of tampon advertisements where women are more active and happier than is reasonable to expect in the circumstances.

'Stop the car!' I shouted at my sister.

I'd seen a chest of drawers. I got out of the car to inspect it. On top, there was a large bag sewn out of denim in the shape of a Santa sack. When I lifted it, I heard rattling sounds. Joy-filled Danish bricks of Lego spilled out on opening – primary-coloured blocks, lots of kits, wheels, tiny windows, astronauts and cowboys. I took the bag and the chest of drawers. I couldn't understand why someone would not have given them to a child who didn't have Lego. An hour later and they would have been landfill. Then came a desk, a chair, a bookshelf – all this, too, would have been landfill. I was not a desperate person scavenging; I was performing a great community service helping to save the planet from more waste. We dropped our stash at my sister's house, had a cup of tea and a Tim Tam, and then drove off again for more looting. We even lifted a foosball table; admittedly, the blue team's right midfielder was missing and the white team's striker was sporting a foot injury, but I knew my daughters would have fun with it. My sister turned up the music. We drove through the cul-de-sacs, laughing like pirates amazed at our booty. We bypassed a piano, lounges, a metal filing cabinet and something that resembled a coffin. We were teenagers again with the windows down, singing as loud as we could to whatever song came on the car radio.

My sister made a U-turn. She'd seen two children's bikes lying across neatly bundled tree clippings and pulled up alongside. I raced out to nab them. As I was positioning the second bike in the car, I thought I heard someone call my name. I ignored it. My name was called again. I looked at the plantation shutters but saw no one. Then I did see her: she was in the doorway. Nadia had been an administrative worker in the health service where I had worked. I had probably earned double what she earned when we worked together about seven years ago. I was hot with embarrassment. She didn't ask questions. She hugged me, said she was pleased to see me, and she offered me boogie boards for my children as well.

Divorce Night Jitters

I had come to feel as confident heading towards my divorce as I had been heading into my marriage. I had been so in love in those days that I'd probably spent five minutes thinking about getting married, but I'd spent five years contemplating ending it.

Even so, I didn't know that to end the marriage with children involved there are three processes. The divorce that ends the marriage, the endorsement of parenting orders and the endorsement of financial orders. The Family Court had on its website that this process would take up to one year; it took us four.

The invitation to my divorce arrived as a white A4 letter from the Family Court, inside an envelope branded with that familiar kangaroo and emu logo. It set the time and date; no mention of a dress code.

Where a wedding is a social event, a divorce is an intensely lonely one. I hadn't told anyone about my appointment except my friend Nicola, who had been my bridesmaid. Sitting together in the cafe outside the court on the appointed morning, even we couldn't talk about it. Instead, we spoke about our kids, school committees and our work. The wedding ivory of the past had given way on this day to a dour suit. My decision to wear a suit seemed obvious once we were actually inside the Family Court building with its grey facade, but I had spent almost as much time deciding what to wear to my divorce as I had spent designing my wedding dress.

Pachelbel's Canon did not herald our entry. There was no music, rousing or soothing, no ritual, no photos and no guests. We entered through the metal detector and placed our bags on a conveyor belt for scanning. Family Court judges had actually had their homes bombed and been killed in the 1980s. The high ceilings were, I suppose, symbolic of the lofty goals of justice, but the cold marble floor where we stood reflected back the bleak reality. Italianate columns that could have reminded me to stand upright, instead made me cower. I felt the weight of judgement pressing down through all the building's features the way European cathedral architects have used scale and stone since medieval times to convince humble potato farmers that they are small and sinful. That a judge decides divorce matters suggests there is some judgement involved.

I wondered if our wedding guests felt ripped off. I did. I knew some of my family members did. I think my family saw more than a correlation in the fact that I was the only family member to be university educated and the only family member to be divorced.

Andrew and I had been following the 'Compulsory Procedures before a Divorce' for the past year. These were as a series of steps along a path, like a pilgrimage leading hopefully to the holy grail of a quick and peaceful resolution. There were many opportunities for penance and self-flagellation along the way. As a social worker, I would have thought the procedures outlined were reasonable. They were, but the starting point to divorce, as the legal definition states, is 'irreconcilable differences', so walking the pilgrim's path could prove anything but peaceful. The destination was clear, but there were few road signs to show the Danger Ahead or to know how long the journey would take.

The first stop was 'Compulsory Family Dispute Resolution'. At our resolution session, in front of the family counsellor, Andrew said he understood the term 'shared parenting' to mean that the children would stay at his house every night. In his vision, I would deliver the children to his house each night when he arrived home from work, after I had picked them up from school at three pm, fed them, helped with homework, driven them to their activities, bathed them and delivered them to his house to sleep. The next morning, he expected that I would pick them up from his house to take them to school after he left for work the next day. His vision of shared parenting brought panic in me. Thankfully, the counsellor brought me up to date on some information that Andrew had already cottoned on to. The amount a parent had to pay to the other parent was based literally on the number of nights the children slept at that house, not the amount of care given. That is why Andrew had developed that proposal. If Andrew's proposal was endorsed, I would do all the parenting tasks, but have no quality time with my children. In his scenario I would only be able to work during school hours, and I would also have to pay him child support because he would be considered to have sole care merely because of the number of nights the children slept at his house. The family counsellor had heard this sort of thing so many times before that she knew we had failed the resolution process, so she shuffled us along the path to the next stop – lawyers. If lawyers could not help us to agree on the amount of time our children spent with each of us, and how our assets should be split, we'd move along the path to the Family Court, who would decide for us. One year into our return from America, we hadn't reached agreement, so divorce was the only business to be completed at the Family Court that day. As sad as I was that our family could not be the ideal I had always wanted, I couldn't wait to no longer be officially associated with Andrew and his behaviour.

Whereas marriages are weekend celebrations, divorces are a bureaucratic weekday business. My workplace allowed leave for moving house, doctors' appointments or attending a funeral, but no time to attend to one's divorce proceedings, so the divorce also cost me a day's pay. The wedding was a moment of strength, a taking of matters into our own hands, with society's trust that we would move forward together. Our divorce was an admission that what we had set out to do did not work. This lack of 'success' in love allowed the Family Court to step in, make determinations for our family and change our lives in all sorts of ways, and yet in other matters, ones that could have helped immeasurably, the Family Court had no power to step in or make decisions.

I saw Andrew as I entered the waiting area. He was seated in a chair, one leg crossed over the other. He looked straight through me. He also ignored Nicola.

We were confined in a space outside the courtroom with about thirty other men and women, penned like cattle waiting to be branded. It wasn't a waiting area, or a quiet area; there was nothing private, or peaceful, or comforting about it. Hearts in transit – like an airport without the excitement, the chatting and the selfies. There were tears and foot pacing and hand wringing. Cardboard cups of water dented too easily in distressed hands. There were a few younger women with their parents, but it looked as though the court served mostly middle-aged women, ten or fifteen years older than me. Nicola and I wondered if they had 'stayed married for the sake of the children'.

Our names were called together, probably for the last time. My husband (as he still was) and I were directed to the back of the courtroom to sit near each other on a wooden bench. Television courtrooms would suggest that family court proceedings feature sassy lawyers with smart arguments and lots of movement, but they don't. We didn't have lawyers. The judge was seated high up, and a ridiculously long way off. We were like naughty children sat up the back of the room.

Because divorce is handled in a legal context and not a social work context, there is no acknowledgement of the hurt and no discussion of feelings. There is no acknowledgement or compensation for broken hearts or broken promises. Divorce creates a much greater need for the support of family and friends than a marriage, but by that time, just like my finances, people I called friends and family had also been reduced by at least half. Perhaps children should be listened to more at this time, and perhaps more should be explained to them. Perhaps children, friends and family should come together at a divorce, like a funeral, and publicly grieve the losses. Perhaps, like a wake, they could share their stories, say farewell to the family in the form it was, make clear their future alliances, and accept without judgement that, as painful as it is, sometimes things change for the better.

*

The judge looked down at the papers. Then she looked over the rim of her round glasses to pointedly address one question to me.

'What have been your sleeping arrangements over the past twelve months?'

Of all the questions that could be asked of a couple with children about to divorce, I couldn't believe that was the vital question that the Family Court needed to know. I saw only the top of her head as she announced officiously, 'In the matter of (our names said together for the last time) I find the documents in order and find the grounds for the granting of a *decree nisi* founded.' She stamped the papers the way bank tellers used to stamp cheques, as the next soon-to-be divorced couple replaced us on the wooden bench.

Creating a New Story

The small bookshelf I had found on the street while fossicking with my sister groaned from the weight of holding books upright and began to sag in the middle. The Harry Potter series, *Charlotte's Web*, *The Little Prince* and other classics, as well as the hard cover picture books they hadn't wanted to part with, had arrived with our other belongings from America. Despite Linda and other friends kindly bestowing on the girls a great literary upbringing, they were at the age where any books that mentioned bums, farts or underpants were preferred. I had to step over *The Bugalugs Bum Thief* on the rug to reach their desk, where I pulled out an exercise book from the drawer. I held it up, knowing this would bring squeals of excitement.

I positioned myself between them on Olivia's bottom bunk. The bed lamp lit their faces. They wore flannelette pyjamas and smelled of oatmeal soap. I smelled of a stressful day at the office. I hadn't yet taken off my work clothes, but I had taken off my bra and replaced my shoes with the QANTAS socks I had kept from our flight home. Feathers that hung from dream catchers licked the top of my head. I used this as an early warning system to avoid my head hitting Sonia's bunk above. White doona hills undulated over our knees. We looked down to quilted squares covering our feet, as if they were fields seen from an aeroplane. From the top of these hills, out of their imaginations popped explorers and astronauts that just happened to often be named Sonia or Olivia. They had been sent on great adventures over mountains, or into space.

Over time, Olivia had been assembling a 'smiling wall' opposite the bed from about ten photographs and a packet of Blu Tack. This was a gallery of snapshots, key moments she'd chosen from six years of life – dance troupes, friendship groups, gymnastic loops and gelato scoops. There was the photograph of Olivia and I dressed as witches for our first Halloween in America, a photo of us all with a snowman during the white Christmas in Lake Tahoe and Ava's favourite was all of us holding on tight at Splash Mountain in Disneyland.

'Let's continue writing our story.'

I asked the girls to think about their bellybuttons. Olivia pushed the doona down towards our knees, kneeled on the bed and turned to face us. She lifted her pyjama top. 'Look at my bellybutton!'

'It looks like there's a tiny bottom stuck in there,' I said.

The girls threw their heads back with laughter.

Sonia joined in: 'Look at mine! Look at mine!'

'Yours looks like a globe of the world,' I said.

We giggled.

'What's yours look like, Mum?'

I untucked my tight white shirt and had to undo some buttons on my black trousers to expose my 'mother belly'. My bellybutton was hidden down a canyon of soft flesh. Both girls brought their heads in close, then moved them back, looking horrified. I quickly squeezed my belly back into my pants, pulled down my shirt and drew their attention back to the exercise book we'd been writing in for the past few nights. We were creating our own story.

I asked them to close their eyes and place their hands on their bellybuttons.

'Focus all your attention there.'

I opened the exercise book and began reading with a grandiose stage voice.

'The Magic Bellybutton by Sonia and Olivia.'

They smiled proudly.

'*Bellybuttons make me laugh. Everyone has one, even my dolls Everyone has one, even my dolls. Not that I still play with dolls, because that's just for babies. Our dogs have lots of bellybuttons, outie bellybuttons, lined up in a row.*'

Giggles.

'*My sister...* What will she be called tonight?' I asked.

'Rita!' Olivia called out.

'Rita? Okay. *Rita has a bellybutton shaped like a bottom. I wonder what having a bellybutton shaped like a bottom means.*'

Loud laughter.

'*Mum says mine is shaped like a globe of the world. That means I'm meant to be a world leader or something.*'

Cackles.

I continued reading: '*Rita and I are twins – which is weird, right, because I thought twins might be joined at the bellybutton. Mum says I was definitely connected to her by my bellybutton when I was in her tummy and that Dad cut the cord that joined our two bellybuttons when I was born. He said it felt like cutting calamari, which is hard to cut, and that's why I eat calamari in one mouthful. Rita and I used to think calamari was a circle fish.*

'*Bellybuttons are very useful. Dad stores lint in his, which apparently is blue stuff and not Mum's favourite brand of chocolate, Lindt. I can't imagine anyone wanting to eat anything that came out of a bellybutton.*'

'Yuk!'

Laughter.

'*Mum says bellybuttons are clever, because they are the same distance from your head and your toes. Spiritual-type people who go to yoga and "yin and yang", think that makes it a powerful part of your body, so they call it "the centre" – dah! They say that if you concentrate really hard on your centre, which is really your bellybutton, you can be powerful and no harm will come to you. So, I know that sounds weird and stuff, but one day I did it. I concentrated really hard on my bellybutton and you won't believe what happened...*

'So, this is the part where we write about the magic bellybutton. What can a magic bellybutton do?' I asked them.

Sonia and Olivia began firing scenarios.

'Sharpen pencils!'

'Cool one!'

'Be a compass if you're lost in the bush!'

'You can store chewing gum in it for later!'

'Yuk!'

They were calling out over the top of one another.

'Beat up bullies,' loudly.

'A tunnel to escape,' louder.

My forearm was tapped repeatedly when one had an idea pop into her head, but the other was already shouting her idea. They were moving around the bed and jostling for attention.

'Orphaned possums can curl up in there for shelter!'
'It could beam like an X-ray!'
'Oh, I know, I know,' Sonia said. 'It could be an ant's pool!'
'Or the bellybutton could turn into a coat hanger.'

This suggestion stumped us all, and when Olivia said it, I knew it was time for bed.

Yawns prevailed, then hugs and good nights.

Sonia climbed the three-rung wooden ladder that connected their bunks. On the wall next to her pillow, she had stuck a colourful drawing of a girl with a smile on her face and a hand coming out of her bellybutton, ready to help. There was a blue sky above and green grass below. Across it she had written, *'Sonia the Super BellyButton Girl!'* We both looked at the picture, then at each other and conspiratorially put a finger over our lips and mouthed a shoosh. Then I kissed her and she tucked herself into bed.

Once they were both settled, I turned off the lights. I gazed up at the luminescent galaxy stickers that I'd stuck to the ceiling. The universe inside our house.

We were three circles on a genogram. Spiritual, magical, divine number three.

Having the girls sleep in bunks meant I could stand and hold each of their hands of slightly different sizes until they became limp, then place their hands back alongside their bodies on the bed. I stayed to watch their caterpillar lashes slowly twitch to stillness. Then there was the reassuring sound of Olivia's snoring.

'Mum,' Sonia whispered once we heard Olivia's snoring.

I had been sure she was asleep. In honesty, I was a little annoyed because I was looking forward to sleeping myself, but I tried not to show it.

'What's up?' I whispered back.

'When I sleep at Dad's house and I cry, Olivia lets me sleep with her on her bed.'

I was glad she was too high up to see the reaction on my face.

'That's very kind of Olivia.'

I stepped on the wooden edge of Olivia's bed to reach her.

Gently stroking her soft cheek with my hand, I told her, 'I know it's hard right now. There's been a lot of changes, but it will get easier, and I'll always be here for you.'

'I know.'

Bronfenbrenner's Babushkas

Everybody has an opinion on how children should be raised. Everybody. And I became one of them – officially, professionally – employed by the New South Wales government to provide parenting advice, sort of. My new role was to synthesise the latest evidence from longitudinal studies, twins studies and brain imaging about children's social, emotional and intellectual development into easily digestible information and practical messages that would also be the basis of a media campaign in five languages.

'What leads to good outcomes for children?' This was the starting point for the project, and the question intrigued me, but as a parent I'd never thought to Google that question. I saw parenting as a relationship. As a single parent, it was my most important relationship, but I didn't see parenting as working to reach an expected outcome. I wasn't trying to make a product and there wasn't a deadline; I knew I was a mother for life.

Although my knowledge and expertise as a social worker and a communicator was what was required in this role, and not my knowledge and experience as a parent, I knew my experience as a parent had given me insights at depths that my knowledge as a professional just couldn't. I didn't know if it was possible to keep my two perspectives (parent and professional) separate in such a role, or if it was even a good thing to try to do.

My professional learning about child development had continued to change. That is, what happened in the womb was once considered to be genetic and fixed, but at the time the womb was beginning to be seen as an environment where genes could be changed, depending on the experiences of the mother. So, nature and nurture were coming closer and closer together, so a child may be born with genes that make that child vulnerable to depression, but it may only be if certain stressful events aggravate those genes that a person would actually become depressed. Without this gene, people who have those same stressful experiences are less likely to become depressed. Research confirmed that what happens in the first years can influence physical health, with conditions such as diabetes and mental health conditions, such as depression in such a way.

*

Russian-American psychologist Urie Bronfenbrenner spent years of his life thinking about the question, 'What leads to good outcomes for children?' He developed a model to show the ways that the child, their family, their community and the values of their society will influence that child's life.

Bronfenbrenner was inspired by Russian babushka (or matryoshka) dolls for his model. These wooden dolls fascinated me as a child because they split apart at the centre to reveal more dolls stacked inside. When all the babushkas are unstacked, the smallest doll at the centre represents the child. The remaining bottom half of the dolls form concentric circles around the child. These circles represent the environments that will influence a child throughout life and the model can show how environments surrounding a child can reinforce or conflict with the values of a family. The closest circle represents the people closest to the child: family, friends and other carers. The organisations that will have the biggest impact on a child, such as school, are in a larger circle, with a circle between them that is meant to show the interrelationships between the parents and the school. An additional circle shows the institutions that can influence a child, but which the child may never come into contact with, namely, a parent's workplace, Family Court or Child Support Agency. These institutions will influence the time parents are available for their children, as well as incomes and stress levels, which of course impact children.

The outermost circle represents the social and political culture in which the child is raised, such as whether the society is secular or religious, patriarchal or matriarchal, and whether that child's family is a member of a disadvantaged group or a privileged group, whether a family are seen as fitting with the norm or different. These factors directly impact the physical and mental health of any family.

Bronfenbrenner's circles suggest that responsibility for good outcomes for children rests with all of us, because children, parents and parenting are intimately connected to the culture and society in which parenting is taking place.

I interpret Bronfenbrenner's circles as showing all the loves a child needs, like the circle of security multiplied on a grander scale. Bronfenbrenner's wise circles, linking child development to everything that happens in the world around a child, leave the shapes in genograms looking naïve in portraying families in isolation from the society around them.

Since returning to Australia as a single parent, it has often felt like we have become trapped in one of Bronfenbrenner's circles, like driving a dodgem car on a circuit round and round at a local fair. Friends and family in our inner circles supported us to power ahead, but some individuals and institutions that were supposed to help actually placed roadblocks in our way. This often left us as the dodgy car without power, stuck at the back of the circuit while other dodgems zoomed past, as if we were invisible.

*

James J Heckman, Professor of Economics at the University of Chicago, showed that what leads to good outcomes for young children also leads to good economic outcomes for a country. He was awarded the Nobel Prize in 2000 for showing that if a government had the choice of investing in building infrastructure, such as roads and airports, or investing early in young children's development, such as providing quality childcare, preschool and supports for vulnerable families, a better raw return on investment comes from targeting that investment towards children. Investing in education and support for families and children gives a ten per cent return, compared with only a seven per cent return for spending on roads and other infrastructure. This is because economic investment in children changes their possible life path from outcomes such as poor school performance, not completing their education, unemployment, crime, drugs and jail (all those potentialities at great cost to the individual, their families and the taxpayer), to the alternative productive path of a good education and a career where they contribute to society.

Heckman's formula influenced countries to spend money on programs for children, but it makes me wonder why countries need to be reassured that it is financially beneficial to care and provide for children before they act.

Despite more evidence and knowledge about what influences children's development, my children's generation are set to be the first to have poorer physical and mental health than their parents. According to the World Health Organization, the children Olivia began kindergarten with will face a greater threat from depression than from any other disease by the time they reach thirty. One in four are predicted to have a mental illness, such as anxiety or schizophrenia, before they become adults, and their unprecedented high levels of obesity could lead them to suffer long-term health problems. These predictions were made prior to the world experiencing the trauma of a global pandemic.

Perhaps the nation needs a care index in the way that we have a share index. Perhaps we could use a care index to monitor the wellbeing of the country's children in the way that we can follow the share index to monitor the health of the country's businesses. A care index might track fluctuations in the support given to children and regular monitoring and resourcing to ensure they are fed, educated, loved and safely tucked in bed each night. Of course, caring for children would involve caring for the carers of children, ensuring they are safe and adequately resourced too.

Broken Homes

'They're from a broken home' was an expression I often heard adults say when I was a child. I wasn't sure what a 'broken home' was, but the tone in which it was said made it clear that it wasn't to be admired. The term was never explained to me, but as a child I thought I knew exactly what it meant. I often saw these broken homes from the backseat of the car, sitting between my brother and sister on road trips with Mum and Dad. Made of wood or asbestos sheeting, these houses were broken clean down the middle and transported on separate trucks to a new location, usually a farm, where the two sides would be reunited and a family would move in. That family would be from a broken home – at least that's what I thought.

As each side of a broken home was too wide for the road it was being transported on, Dad would be forced to pull over into the stretch of dusty track bordering the bitumen and wait for the flatbed trucks carrying their half homes to pass us. The flashing lights announced WIDE LOAD FOLLOWING. Seated between my brother and sister, I'd feel the anticipation build until we caught sight of the oversized truck transporting the first half of the house. These broken homes intrigued me. I wondered what had happened to break them and how they would be glued back together.

The inside of each half of the home was totally exposed. There would always be something specific inside that we were anxious to see, but we were never sure if it was going to be in the first half of the broken home or the second half. We squashed against windows and tried covering each other's eyes in order to win at the game of being the first to see it. Then my brother, being more capable at these methods than my sister and me, would yell, 'I see it!' Then he'd punch me in the arm. I never understood why he did that, when we'd been having such fun. If I complained about him punching me, my Mum would say, 'Stop being so sensitive' and my Dad would say 'Stop it or I'll give you something to cry about'.

The wonder we were waiting for was the toilet. As the wide loads passed, there it would be in plain sight, sitting high in the middle of the bathroom.

'Like a throne,' my mother would say. We'd laugh as it moved along the freeway.

'Someone's sitting on it!' my brother would joke. This would send us into such rapturous laughter that we almost needed that toilet ourselves.

It was bizarre to see a stationary, private object like a toilet roving through the countryside with pomp and purpose, forcing other cars off the road to wait for its passing, as if it really were a throne with a royal sitting on top. The toilet was often the only fixture in one half of the broken home, the private area of the house exposed for everyone to see. It was then that I understood why being from a broken home was such a bad thing. As a child, I reasoned that broken homes exposed things that should be kept private.

I thought 'broken home' was a term that only my father's generation used like 'sheila' or 'no hoper'. I certainly hadn't heard it since my childhood. But since we'd been back in Australia, I'd heard friends say 'broken home' when they were speaking about other families in our situation: 'They're also from a broken home.' These same friends had been wonderfully helpful to us, so I assumed they must not think the term sounded like it was something inferior.

This reflects the lack of suitable terms to refer to any family that does not appear in the shape of the nuclear family. The Child Support Agency refers to all its clients, as 'separated', even though we are divorced and some of its clients may have never lived together. The Australian Bureau of Statistics refers to our family as a 'one-parent family', even though my children have two parents. Instead of two parents, my children have two single parents.

Harry Potter author JK Rowling once said, 'I am prouder of my years as a single mother than of any other part of my life.' She has spoken about the stigma of being a single parent and the treatment she received by the social support system. I haven't written a Harry Potter series, nor am I one of the world's richest women, but I agree with JK Rowling in that I, too, am prouder of my years as a single mother than of any other part of my life. And yet I was not one to advertise my status as a sole parent, for fear that I would be seen as a lesser parent or a lesser professional. This was especially so when I was employed to provide information to parents about what leads to good outcomes for children. Throughout this work, I read studies concluding that I was a lesser parent because I wasn't parenting with a father in the house. I read about myself as a member of a group that has been psychologically and sociologically prodded and poked by researchers looking for faults, looking for weakness, looking for difference – pitting the work and resources of one parent against the work and resources of two parents. The problem with this research is that its starting point was the question, 'How are children in single-parent families worse off than children in married families?'

Psychological studies of single parents were originally driven by a cultural assumption that only one family type was desirable. Anything outside of a nuclear heterosexual family, where the father worked and the mother was the sole carer of children, it was assumed would negatively impact children simply because it was not the cultural ideal. Experts developed this into family-deficit theory. The research that had been gathered over the years supported this approach.

Family-deficit theory then influenced policies and practices that were enforced by governments. It played out in extreme practices that saw unmarried pregnant women coerced into surrendering their babies for adoption to more suitable two-parent families. Further judgements about acceptable families, coupled with racism, shockingly led to generations of Aboriginal children being forcibly removed from their families to be placed with white families, or into institutions. The traumatic impacts of these policies on individuals and families are still being felt today.

Experts at the time argued that such policies were 'in the best interests of the children'. I am worried by the possibility that if I had trained as a social worker decades earlier when such views prevailed, could I have been taught to think like this. If I had followed the professional knowledge, policies and practices of the time, could I have possibly supported the taking of children from their families because of the colour of their skin? If I had been a mother as well as a social worker at the time, could I possibly have done that to another mother and child?

*

Accuracy matters in research, but I have noticed that studies are not precise in their definitions of the single-parent groups they study. They fail to capture the range of experiences of single-parent families or the married families they compare them with. These studies have not made clear whether the single-parent families in their studies had always been single, or whether children had experienced their parents' divorce or a death of a parent. These factors could impact children differently and could be seen to be more impactful at certain times than the structure of their family. Most single parents, like myself, probably never planned to be – given that seventy per cent of single parents were once married or in a long-term de facto relationship. When studies refer to single parents, they usually mean children living with their mother. They are rarely explicit about the father's involvement in such families, but obviously this has an impact.

American studies have shown that those who grew up in single parent families with adequate resources tend to do well. Children who received financial supports from the father, did better than those that didn't and this showed in improvements in standardised test scores with every $100 of child support a child received. The same study found that children of single mothers who have contact and emotional support from their fathers tend to do better than those with no contact with their fathers.

Research is moving on from the question, 'How are children in single-parent families worse off than children in married families?', which only served to judge and shame. Now they tend to ask a more helpful question: 'What have been the factors in single-parent families that have led to children's success?' This research elicits far more useful answers.

I was comforted to find, in the research that started with this question, that at least one stable, loving adult in a child's life is enough for a child to have positive outcomes. The research also found that it doesn't matter if this supportive person is male or female – it's the love and support that counts, not the gender. That supportive person doesn't even need to be a parent, it might be a grandparent, family friend or teacher. This paints a far more positive view and knowing these positive factors are vital for parents, because self-efficacy (a parent's own belief in themselves as capable to perform the job required of them) is another important protective factor for children growing up.

Most single mothers work and, even while working, many don't earn enough to stay above the poverty line. Even if a lone mother could work full time, at the same time as raising children, it is to be expected that she will earn 14.2 per cent less than her male counterpart, solely on the basis that she is a woman. This is thanks to an acknowledged national gender pay gap calculated using Australian Bureau of Statistics data. This data has shown that in 2021, for every dollar a man earns full-time, on average, a woman also working full-time earns only 86 cents. For the same time at work each week, women earned $261.50 less than a man and $13,000 less in a year. When the part-time workforce is added, the total earnings gender pay gap for all employees widens to 31.3 per cent. This means women's average weekly total earnings are $486.20 less than men's. It is likely that my daughters will still experience this, as it is expected to take more than a century to close the full-time total renumeration gender pay gap completely, according to the report *Gender Equity Insights 2021: Making it a Priority* written by Bankwest Curtin Economics Centre and the Workplace Gender Equality Agency.

This difference in pay affects women throughout their working life, but also as they age, because they will have accumulated less assets and superannuation. Men will retire on 30 per cent more than women. This does not even factor in any time out of the workforce to raise children.

A consistent finding from reams of evidence for more than one hundred years is that poverty and disadvantage are the main barriers to successful outcomes for children. It is this factor that can be the biggest difference between single-parent families and families with two parents. Divorce can send women towards poverty and keep them there for the rest of their lives if they have been caring for children. Lone-mother families are three times more likely than any other family group to be living in poverty. In Australia, someone in the highest income group will receive around five times as much income as someone in the lowest income group. Because a third of sole-parent families live in poverty, it is easy for the two factors – poverty and single parenthood – to be conflated.

I was aware of my privilege, as a white, educated woman with a home. My tertiary education has meant that I have been employable and capable of supporting my family. It has meant that I could navigate complex systems and advocate for myself or my children when needed. It was as if my two degrees had been fashioned into a little paper boat that allowed us to bob about on the water, not steaming forward, but not needing to bail.

I'd had quite enough of people researching single parents who had no understanding of what it is like to be a single parent, with book knowledge but no common sense, as my parents would say. I'd had quite enough of studies that told me that, as a single mother, my parenting must be found wanting. All the single mothers I knew were resilient and capable and I wanted to read their stories and hear their voices. There were books in the social work, psychology, sociology and even self-help section where single mothers had been written about by others. There were motherhood memoirs often written by famous mothers who had husbands, but I couldn't find books actually written by single parents. Not one book came to mind as I looked in the autobiography section at my local library. I asked the librarian, who was also at a loss to suggest something.

'We mostly stock autobiographies written by politicians and war heroes,' she said.

The Year of Upside Downs

Olivia declared the year she turned eight to be the Year of Upside Downs. On the day of the declaration, I was standing before the full-length mirror in my bedroom, dressing for work. I could see her reflection in the mirror behind me – her hands where her feet should be, and her feet where her hands should be. Her long brown hair was skimming the floorboards. Her knees were bent backwards over my bed, her flannelette pyjama top yawning with gravity to reveal her pale-skinned belly. Olivia's preference that year was to spend her time in a handstand, walkover or cartwheel. She assessed people from the ground up, paying particular attention to their shoes.

In the Year of Upside Downs, Olivia folded paper into a cube and reinforced the sides with sticky tape to make a die. She had learnt that the sides of the die are called faces, so on each she drew a face – mine, hers, Sonia's, the faces of our new puppies, Midnight and Daylight, and Shelby, one of our five white rabbits. She instructed us that she would throw the die each morning and whoever's face was on top would be in charge of the house for that day. That person or animal would have the power to tell everyone what they could and couldn't do. Olivia and Sonia had separate rooms by this time, so the die toss happened in Olivia's room, so only Olivia (and occasionally Daylight) would witness the result. Olivia would then announce the outcome to the rest of the house. Needless to say, I won the toss as infrequently as the number of times I rolled a six playing Trouble (the number needed to start moving along the path in that boardgame). Sonia fared no better. Our dogs, Midnight and Daylight, won the die toss a lot.

Midnight, a border collie cross cattle dog, and Daylight, a kelpie mix, were emboldened by winning the die toss and worked as a team to eat through each other's leather collars. In the backyard, I watched Midnight stand still as a post as she offered Daylight a clear passage to gnaw at her collar until she was freed from bondage. They preferred to eat when they wanted, often helping themselves to whatever I had just cooked, cupcakes or mini quiches left on the bench to cool down. From the beginning, we intended to train them, but the only dog-training school in our area required each dog to have a child over twelve years with an adult present. We didn't have another adult and the girls weren't over twelve, so our dogs didn't progress beyond puppy preschool. Our untrained dogs somehow chewed and clawed their way through the back wall at the bottom of the house, which had been damaged by a leaking pipe. On the inside of this wall was a bookshelf, and I came home from work one day to find Midnight sharpening her teeth on my hardcover art book of Frida Kahlo prints. Daylight was similarly appreciating Jane Austen. They found so many items on which to strengthen their teeth and claws that year, I worried that they would dig up the pets that had gone before them that lay buried in the backyard.

I had initially been steadfast in resisting the emotional pleas for a dog. As a substitute for a real dog, we'd watch *Inspector Rex*, a police dog who solved crimes in both Italian and German police stations. I finally agreed to us having a dog when I read that dogs improve their owners' health. I imagined playing dog Frisbee with other clever canines at the park. Then I discovered the cost of those genetically engineered designer dogs that don't shed fur or do anything wrong. We couldn't afford one of those, so instead we rescued two puppies. We left the shelter with two puppies because the girls couldn't agree on which dog they wanted. Once in the car, Midnight did a sloppy poo that sat like a puddle of gravy on the floor at Sonia's feet. This made Sonia vomit, which led Daylight to jump from Olivia's lap in the front seat to the backseat to start eating the vomit. I was already questioning the research findings that dogs improve their owners' health.

Prior to that, we had bought two white rabbits, Shelby and Chuppa Chup, from a local family who told us they were sisters. In the Year of Upside Downs, we discovered they weren't sisters when they became parents to three baby rabbits, which Sonia and Olivia named Dumper, Thumper and Yawning Jumper. So, when Shelby won the die toss, Olivia took Shelby's turn to be leader of the house, given that Shelby had family responsibilities to attend to.

In the Year of Upside Downs, unlike Shelby, I spent Mother's Day without my children and it felt like I was the only mother ever to do so. I had once looked upon Mother's Day cynically, as a day created to sell chrysanthemums, kitchen appliances and slippers, but since becoming a mother, it had taken on a new significance. Despite the commercial push surrounding it, in the suburb where I lived, there was always a genuine atmosphere of love and acknowledgement for the role of caregiving on this day. I had begun to like how the countdown to Mother's Day animated my daughters, making them think of creative ways to show their love. One year, Sonia made good use of her pen licence to write an acrostic poem in red pen on yellow paper for my Mother's Day card:

LYNN
L: *Lovely*
Y: *Yodelling*
N: *Nice*
N: *Neat*

I know that only having the letter y instead of a vowel made it difficult, but in receiving such cards, I understood more about how my daughters saw me, and the urgent need to boost their vocabulary.

What excited me most was the anticipation of the gifts they bought from the school Mother's Day stall. I remember how excited I was as a child choosing a gift for my own mother at one of these stalls.

My children could choose from an array of candles, soaps or kitchen wares, displayed on trestle tables. They cost twenty dollars. The mothers who would be receiving these gifts had volunteered their time collecting money, purchasing presents, wrapping, arranging them and helping the children to choose what their mother might like. These mothers would do it all again in four months' time for Fathers' Day.

*

Also that year, the Family Court enacted its power to determine the amount of money I should pay Andrew to settle the financial orders. In the Year of Upside Downs, I ended in a worse financial situation than when I had entered the marriage, with no hope of regaining my position or income from that time, while I remained the main carer for two children. On the upside, after four years of waiting for this determination in the Family Court, I could begin to make plans. There was great comfort in knowing we didn't have to move house, but it did mean I had to find a better-paid job in order to meet the cost of paying Andrew his proportionate cost of the house.

The Family Court also enacted its power to determine the amount of time our children could spend with each of us. The court-endorsed arrangements finally offered hope for peace and stability, compared to the years before, when decisions about which parent the children would stay with might as well have been decided by Olivia's die toss.

The parenting orders made clear arrangements for special days, like Mother's Day, that would override the usual custody arrangements. We had negotiated that our daughters would spend four hours with me in the daytime on Mother's Day if it was the weekend they normally spent with their father, and vice-versa on Father's Day, if it fell on the weekend they spent with me. Both Andrew and I were to carve up Christmas, Easter and children's birthdays equally. For our children, time was a magic pudding that had to keep giving. In the Year of Upside Downs, Mother's Day fell on the weekend they were with their father, but he refused to drive Olivia and Sonia to my house at the designated time.

'You come and get them,' he said on the phone. I would have done so, except that I had fractured the right lateral malleolus in my ankle and I couldn't put my foot on the pedal to drive. In the Year of Upside Downs, it became clear that the Family Court had no power to enforce its own parenting orders.

My extended family were having a Mother's Day get-together, and I was invited but had no way of getting there. So, it looked as though I wouldn't see my children or my mother on Mother's Day. Relations with my family had been strained since the first Christmas after our return to Australia, when a member of my extended family wanted to invite my ex-husband, and asked, 'Why can't you be a normal family for once?' Family ties loosened at the very time I wished they could have tightened.

On that Mother's Day, I sat on the lounge with my leg propped on cushions and wrapped with ice in a tea towel featuring koalas (thanks to last year's Mother's Day stall). The lounge extended along the window, where I looked out to the gum tree. I'd recently had the branches lopped to reduce the threat of them falling. I watched the slender branches move with the wind as the birds came and went. The clouds moved too, but the trunk remained as still as I was. From where I sat, I could see the jacaranda, where my children liked to swing on the tyre attached to its branches, and I ached for their touch. In one corner of the aluminium window frame, I watched a spider roll its dinner between lanky grey legs. Nearby, in a softly matted web, it looked like hundreds of baby spiders had popped their eggs and run away from their mother in all directions, forming a small grey cloud. I did not spray them.

*

For some reason, at my lowest point, I thought it a good idea to start Googling Mother's Day. I was surprised to find it had developed during the American Civil War. The Mother's Day Proclamation was an appeal by mothers to demand that countries stop wars that destroyed families. Somehow, from its peace activist beginnings, Mother's Day had become the equivalent of Valentine's Day for women with children.

I also found on the internet that in Australia, the Mother's Day gift-giving tradition began when a concerned woman, Janet Heyden, brought gifts to poor mothers at a home for women in Parramatta back in the 1920s. It made me think that if I had been alive then, as a single mother, I might well have been one of those women she was visiting.

*

Sadly, in the year of Upside Downs, my friend Georgette passed away and she was greatly missed by me and my children. Over the years she had quietly accepted each new limitation to her life. Despite the hundreds of people at her funeral, few would have known that she had been part of a loving partnership, but she felt she could never let her family know this. She had never even felt free enough to hold her partner's hand walking down the street where she lived for fear of shame. In her final days, about to be freed of the disease that was denying her oxygen, she could not be free to receive the love and support from her partner, for fear of losing the love and support of her family.

*

The ability to get through the polite conversations before, during and after Mother's Day – 'Did the children make you breakfast in bed?' – required all my strength. Cafes burst with three generations of family on Mother's Day in my suburb, so being without my children on this day felt like ostracism on the scale that came with finding nits in your child's hair. I didn't call anybody, and nobody called me, which was probably for the best.

On my solo Mother's Day, I watched the sky bruise outside my window, as it turned from blue to pink, orange, purple, then black. The baby spiders dispersed. The ice that was rehabilitating my ankle melted and fell to the carpet alongside the wet tissues and chocolate wrappers scattered over the floor where I was sitting.

I was taken by surprise when the doorbell rang. I reached for my crutches and quickly binned the chocolate wrappers and the tissues as I passed the kitchen bin on my way to the front door.

'Happy Mother's Day!' Sonia and Olivia jumped at me, almost pushing me off the crutches. I saw Olivia holding a present. The girls began to squabble over who should be the first to give me their gift. They usually came home bickering after a weekend at Dad's and it often took them until after school on Monday afternoon to properly settle again. Other parents said the transition at their house each week was the same. Swapping between houses with different sets of rules and wading through the emotional puddle in the middle must have been incredibly difficult for my daughters.

Sonia ran to her room, yelling back, 'I've got the best present for you, Mum.'

'Sonia hasn't really got the best present,' Olivia retorted and stayed for a hug.

'Seeing you two is the best present ever.'

'Guess what I got you for Mother's Day,' Olivia said.

I could see clearly what it was through the cellophane, but I played along. 'Is it something for the kitchen?'

'Noooooo.' She shook her head.

'Is it something for the bathroom?'

'No, no, guess, guess.' She was jumping up and down.

'Is it flowers?'

'C'mon, Mum.'

Olivia had spent the week before Mother's Day hinting at the wonderful present she had for me, and I had spent it trying to guess what the present could be. One of the other school mothers, Sue Finch, who worked the Mother's Day stall, had told me that an older boy was about to lift that present off the large trestle table when Olivia snatched it, almost taking it from his hands, saying, 'Mum will love this.'

In the doorway, the anticipation became too much and Olivia, almost shivering with excitement, burst out, 'It's Beldrum!' She looked calmer after that. Beldrum was a type of green gnome or the result of a cross breeding experiment between a garden gnome and a wizard. He was made of plaster or whatever gnomes are made of. He was dressed in green and red, like an elf, and was thin with a pointy hat. He had a beard made of soft white down like the fur on the underbelly of our rabbits, and he was playing a guitar. Not being a particular fan of garden gnomes, it reminded me again, that I really should share more about myself with my daughters.

'Thank you. What a wonderful present!'

I bent down awkwardly on my crutches and hugged her again.

'Mum?'

'Yes?' Still bent, looking into Olivia's steel-grey eyes. 'Will Santa bring presents when we're at Dad's house this year?'

'Yes, of course.'

She thought for a while.

'Mum?'

'Yes, Olivia?'

'Will Santa still bring presents when we're at your house?'

'Yes, of course.'

'Mum?'

'Yes?'

'I feel sorry for kids that only live at one home.'

'Do you? Why?'

'Because Santa and the Easter Bunny only come to them once.'

I smiled and I hugged her. 'You're right, you're lucky to have two homes.'

'Yes, I know.'

I watched her turn to enter her bedroom, calling, 'Soniaaaaa... Your turn to give Mum her present.'

Work/Life Wheel

I'm swimming, swimming, with arms arcing over my head to enter the icy blue water, but I'm like a child with weak, skinny arms that don't pull through the water. Dragged back, I have to swim faster or I'll be late to pick up Sonia, but something is holding me down and the cold, salty water is in my mouth, making it feel wide and loose like I can't control it to scream or to keep the fishy waves from swirling in and filling it up. I'm scared, so very scared, I'm alone and I'm worried I'll be late, but my director in a suit is under the water holding my leg. Suddenly, Olivia is there in a boat. She couldn't get to school because I forgot to sign a note and I'm gulping air and I have to pick up Sonia, but I can't get out of work…

*

My eyes were wide open in the darkness when I realised I had stopped breathing. My breath remained pinned against the wall of my chest. I opened my mouth, lurching my body back and forth trying to dislodge it. Nothing. I repeated the

Work/Life Wheel

action. Nothing. I clutched at my throat. Then my breath gushed out like water from a drain freed of debris, but something remained pressing on my heart, causing me pain with each breath. It felt like it could have been an antique flatiron used for pressing wrinkles from linens. It felt like it was pressing wrinkles from my scrunched-up heart.

The flatiron continued its work as I made breakfasts, packed lunches, braided hair, fed dogs, took my daughters to school and gave them an extra-large hug. Then I drove myself to hospital. The emergency department was the last place I'd seen Dad after he had died from a heart attack. They laid me flat. Nurses descended. Ripped at clothes. Bellowed instructions. Pushed monitors from patient to patient. I noticed everyone who worked in the emergency ward wore running shoes and everyone ran.

I worried about calling work to say I'd be late. I'd been working full time at a more bureaucratic, better-paid job for the past five years. Again, I was employed to write parenting resources, but by a different government department. We were one team, but the office politics literally divided the office in half. It was the sort of workplace where colleagues talked about you behind your back. In your absence, they'd talk about your work, what you were wearing, who you'd spoken to or what you'd said. When you returned, the friendly colleagues would repeat to you what had been said about you. I'd stay at work longer and during lunch, just to avoid being spoken about. Some of my colleagues had begun taking anti-anxiety medication. The office was in an iconic colonial sandstone building and, not surprisingly, it stood next to the park where convicts had been flogged when Sydney was a penal colony. A decorative cupola projected out of the top floor. The sunlight that beamed in illuminated the official receptions, training sessions and seminars held there.

Under the cupola, I attended a seminar where the CEO encouraged women to apply for senior roles. 'At least there is no glass ceiling in our organisation.' The ceiling may or may not have been glass, but the floor beneath me felt very sticky.

'How can you take on a more senior role if you want access to family-friendly work arrangements?' said one of the directors I reported to, when I asked about applying for a role that was available.

He greeted me each morning with 'good afternoon', when I arrived an hour after him, despite the fact I was well within the flexible starting times our workplace promoted. After I fed my children, signed notes, found gold coins for Mufti Day – or waited until seven to drive to the 7-Eleven to buy milk as a way to gather gold coins for Mufti Day – made healthy breakfasts and lunches, got myself ready, waited for the school playground to be opened, drove to the station and commuted forty-five minutes, I arrived at work following a twelve-minute sprint-walk in professional heels. Sometimes, overnight, some wildlife had wandered into our backyard and the dogs might have mauled to death a possum, a blue-tongue lizard or a red-bellied black snake, and I would have to collect the ripped, stiff anatomical pieces looking at me in horror and bury them in the garden, or bag them and bin them. I imagine that, in contrast, before work my manager would have woken up and caught the ferry.

My workplace had won awards for the flexible work entitlements they offered, but these were totally left to the discretion of directors.

'It's a policy, not an entitlement' was all that needed to be said to end the discussion.

In our open-plan office, my work colleagues rolled their eyes if I briefly called my children after school on the days they were in their father's care to check they had reached his house, even though my colleagues often called their partners. At one point, Andrew just left for a six-week European trip without telling me beforehand, and hadn't really put in place any plans for his days of care while he was away. On these days, they had to come back to my house while I was at work. I took to calling to check on their welfare in the stairwell or the toilet so as not to disturb anyone. During one of these days, a work colleague I thought was a friend had sent an email, not intended for me but written about me, sent to me by mistake, with something unkind to say about me spending too much time in the toilet. I had worked so hard to follow precisely the working-mother obligation as outlined by Annabel Crabb in *The Wife Drought*: '…that one ought to work as if one did not have children, while raising one's children as if one did not have a job.'

*

The nurses yelled.
'What's your name?'
'How old are you?'
'Who's your next of kin?'
Their voices got louder each time.
I knew well enough my name and age, but I didn't know whose name to give as next of kin. I didn't want the hospital to inform my daughters of bad news. I didn't want my mother to come to the hospital and see me in that state. I gave them a friend's contact details instead.

*

'Perhaps you shouldn't start work so early,' had been the school principal's response to a request I made with a group of parents for outside-of-school-hours care to be provided at the school.

'If you're so busy working, why did you take on the role of president of the School Council?'

I had taken on the role of president of the School Council to lobby for outside-of-school-hours care. If our school had had that option like other schools did, it could have opened employment opportunities for many families, and primarily helped women to continue their careers, because our days would not have been dictated by the three pm pick up. The principal opposed it at every opportunity. Outside-of-school-hours care finally opened after he left the school, in the year my youngest daughter left for high school.

*

Nurses tattooed my chest with white circular stickers and attached electrodes. I thought they were put there to send electric shocks to start my heart if the blip on the monitor flatlined. When the heart monitor determined that I was not having a heart attack, the staff raced with their high-octane-fuelled energy to a new patient. Rather than a stent or a transplant, I was given a sedative and a comfort teddy supplied by the Red Cross.

*

Working full time meant I was often needed in two places at once on opposite sides of Sydney. I couldn't be there because of traffic, or because of work, or because I had a problem saying 'no'. I definitely had a problem saying 'no' to the groups who wanted volunteers to cook barbecues, sell raffle tickets and bake cakes so the school could buy equipment. Also, there was a requirement that if you were paying for your child to be in the school band, you would make yourself available to volunteer with band set-up, marking the roll, supervising students and packing the equipment away before school started. The mums collating the lists of volunteers sometimes used school newsletters or group emails to shame parents who didn't regularly attend to these duties. On weekends I had to compulsorily 'volunteer' at the soccer canteen, regardless of whether it was actually my weekend with my children or not. The volunteer-recruiters didn't hassle Andrew to work at the canteen. Instead, when they saw him on the sideline at his daughter's game, they'd say what a great dad he was to come and watch his daughter play.

*

I was wheeled on a noiseless trolley to the back lot of the emergency ward, where the pace was less frenetic. I knew this to be the bay where social workers collected the still-breathing bodies rejected from the nurses and doctors to be moved on to family, friends or an aged care facility. Plastic pneumatic doors separated this area for the chronic and long term from the acute in emergency. Like a puppy in a dog-rescue shelter, each time the doors opened, my hopes rose in expectation that it was someone to take me home. In reality, I had driven myself, so I had to take myself home.

*

I tried, but I couldn't keep up the neighbourhood standard of garbage bins having to be disinfected, wheeled back in and straightened every Monday before leaving for work. My fence palings didn't remain upright, the spiders weren't sprayed and the leaves weren't bullied into a pile with a jet engine blower that rumbled through what could otherwise be a quiet Sunday sleep-in.

I felt guilty that one daughter had to stop ballet lessons because I couldn't be home at four in the afternoon to put her hair into the tight bun the ballet school required. And I didn't know how I had allowed one child to expect to be driven to gymnastics, thirty minutes from home, twice a week, at the same time that I had led my other child to expect that I could drive her to netball, twenty minutes in the opposite direction. So, I understand that I, along with other 'soccer mums', am responsible for Sydney's traffic problems. This report finding was announced on a radio news segment I heard as I was driving my daughter to maths tutoring. It could be true, because I also drove forty minutes in peak hour for one daughter's flute tutoring, and they both played soccer on weekends for different teams at ovals across Sydney. As well, there was band practice and clarinet lessons and the activities for the Duke of Edinburgh challenge. I knew that involvement in such activities was a protective factor for children's wellbeing, boosting their mental and physical health, but it had the opposite effect on mine.

Had I become the contemporary archetype of the 'good' mother, conforming to unrealistic ideals against which mothers are both judged and judge themselves? Notably these same standards are not applied to fathers. If I organised to take a day of my annual leave to attend a school performance, I read that I was a helicopter mum, hovering over my children. I read also that because I was a divorced, single mother, I was probably compensating for something my children were missing.

*

Perhaps I had Verbraekennised my children just like my childhood friend Tanya's parents had done to her. Perhaps the Verbraekenns would be considered Tiger Mums (I haven't heard of an equivalent term for Dads) if they were parenting these days. Maybe I was expecting too much in encouraging my child to sit the state's selective high school exam with thirteen thousand other students for one of only four thousand places. I looked over the practice exam papers and the questions were overwhelming I thought for an 11-year-old:

In a foreign language MACHE ARCA KIP means SMALL MAGICAL CARDS, and MACHE FLO ROT means TRICKS IN CARDS. If GO FUP LECTY means SMOKE AND DISAPPEAR and FLO means IN, which of the following means MAGICAL CARDS DISAPPEAR IN SMOKE?
a. ARCA KIP FLO FUP GO
b. MACHE LECTY FUP FLO ROT
c. MACHE ARCA ROT FUP LECTY
d. ARCA MACHE FLO LECTY FUP

Although Sonia was in the top maths class at her school, her teacher explained that everyone else in the class was tutored, so if I didn't pay for a tutor, she would fall behind.

In two years' time, Olivia would be entering high school too, so we spent weeknights 'school shopping' again, just as we had for Sonia. Along with every other family in Sydney, we attended high school open days in the belief that we were choosing the best school for our child, not realising that the schools were really the ones doing the choosing. My parents had certainly never performed all of these services for me. And yet, one thing I had wished for my children was to offer them opportunities I didn't have. Even when high school shopping, it was hard to know how much was caring enough and how much was caring too much.

I had read studies that showed being kind to just one person leads others (even people you will never come into contact with) to be kind to others. They found that being altruistic magnifies and pays forward. It follows then that a parent's altruism – their expression of loving kindness towards their child with no expectation of reward – may be the best thing a parent can do for their own personal happiness (not only their child's). Neuroscientists recording Buddhist monks' brain activity while they meditated confirm that even meditating on altruism makes people happy. These Tibetan monks recited a centuries-old loving-kindness meditation that focuses on altruistic love, compassion and forgiveness, particularly for those who have wronged us. Their brains produced gamma waves, creating feelings of peace and happiness.

The health benefits of altruism, however, seem to escape divorced single mothers. Research conducted on twenty-five thousand women from a range of countries by the Harvard Center for Population and Development Studies found that single motherhood is associated with poorer health and disability in later life than that experienced by women with partners. It found that single mothers are more likely to suffer from depression and mental ill health even after their socio-economic position is accounted for. The study also found that women who divorced appeared to face worse health outcomes at older ages than those who have children outside of marriage or are widowed.

In Australia, the average divorced woman has assets valued at ninety per cent less than her married equivalent, and divorced women earn ten per cent less than their married equivalents. A newly single mother often finds it hard to make ends meet, particularly if she is the primary carer of the former couple's children. She may take low-paid jobs due to family-friendly hours. It may take five years to recover from the financial impact of divorce and there remains a twenty per cent gap in the financial wellbeing of divorced and married couples even after six years. The Child Support Agency clearly had not taken this information into account in the formulas they developed for the cost and care percentage of each parent.

Whereas once I might have collected such statistics to write into an issues paper, or a policy document, or to request a grant, I found myself in a position where I was actually living these statistics. As a social worker, I could speak eloquently about the inequalities of such a position and be an effective advocate, but being one of these statistics left me in a far less powerful position.

One daughter, unaware of these statistics, slammed her bedroom door (which broke) because I had 'ruined her life' by forgetting to sign an excursion note before I left for work. I asked my other daughter if she could please place her dirty washing *in* the washing pile, not just *next* to it. She responded with, 'I can't do everything at the same time.'

*

I watched the plastic hospital doors open pneumatically each time a green button was pressed, and my hope for some assistance jumped each time a health professional entered. The pain across my chest remained. I noticed that I could no longer turn my head towards the right. My body felt as if it was bound tight from the inside out, as if each organ had been restrained, the stomach so tight I couldn't enjoy eating food, the lungs restricting the movement of breath.

The emergency staff ran at such a frenetic pace, they pushed through the plastic doors before the pneumatics had fully opened them. There was only one staff member I saw who waited calmly, allowing the doors their agency before she sauntered through. Her white soft-soled shoes moved along the white linoleum floor towards me, giving the illusion that she floated. Her brown, wavy hair sat around her broad shoulders. She placed her blue social work diary and pager on the bed and warmed my cold hands in hers. She introduced herself as Angelica.

She asked me what was happening in my life. Then she listened. When I finished, she opened a page at the back of her diary left blank for notes. She drew a circle divided into equal-sized segments, the way I used to in explaining fractions to my children, but in her diagram, each segment represented a fraction of life: work, family, personal growth, health and wellbeing, romance and friends. I knew this as the work/life wheel. It could be used as a tool to help people get some balance in their life by identifying how they spend their time.

She placed the numbers one to ten along each spoke of the wheel, number one at the centre, number ten at the outer rim. She asked me to draw a line across each segment at the height of the number that best represented the amount of time I spent on that aspect of my life. If I had apportioned my time

Work/Life Wheel

adequately in all areas of my life, I would have drawn a perfect wheel that turns the way it was intended.

My drawing instead showed a line hitting the height of the number ten only on the family and work segments; all other segments registered a one or a two, and so my wheel ballooned out at two sides.

'Your tyre is flat.'

'I can't stop working.'

'Work and family are huge responsibilities in your life and you are not supported in either of these roles right now.'

'I have to -'

Angelica interrupted: 'Lynn, you cannot continue like this.' She tightened her hand around mine, looked me in the eye and, with a subtlety more suited to policing than social work, she said, 'Lynn, think of your daughters. If you continue like this, you won't be there for them and then what will they do?'

Paris with Loner Issues

I took Angelica's advice, well at least the way I interpreted it. I cashed in all my leave at work and booked an overseas holiday. The end of proceedings in the Family Court after four years meant that Sonia and Olivia could again have passports. During court proceedings, Andrew had refused to sign the paperwork to renew their passports, using this as a bargaining chip until the settlement.

I wanted to take my daughters far away from our suburban routines. Routines that had to ensure I was safely inside my house when their father parked in my driveway, despite Family Court orders instructing him not to park in my driveway. He sometimes parked my car in as I was leaving, or knocked at my door when he dropped the girls off at random times. For six whole weeks I would have time with my daughters that wasn't broken into predetermined days and nights spent at Mum's house or Dad's house. For six weeks I could live without him bullying me to accept arrangements he wanted. I wanted to give my daughters the opportunity to reconnect with their friends in America and I wanted to thank our friends over there who had been so generous and helped when I needed it. I wanted to offer my daughters a cultural tour through which to sample the world, round out their education, and share with them the art, architecture and history I had enjoyed on previous travels. But mostly I wanted us to just have fun.

When I told people about our plans, the first reaction was, 'How can you afford that?' When these same families talked excitedly about their travel plans, I didn't ask about their finances; I said, 'How wonderful! Have a great holiday!'

These families knew I worked full time. They might not have known I cashed in all my leave and that we planned to stay with friends in Kuala Lumpur, Latvia and LA on our travels. They might not have known that, when they bought their HDTVs the size of billboards for their home cinemas, we had lived without a television ever since Chuppa Chup won the die toss in the Year of Upside Downs because, with his winning toss, he chose to run free inside the house and he ate through the electrical cord attached to the television as if it was a carrot. I asked the girls if they wanted to spend money on a new TV or if they wanted to spend it on our overseas holiday, and they decided on the holiday. To reach their savings goal for the trip, the girls busked at the local shopping centre, playing flute and clarinet with their friends.

Andrew signed the required paperwork, stating that he allowed the children to leave the country with me. I also had to complete a form for the Department of Education, outlining special reasons for removing the children from school for four weeks of the school term. I emphasised the educational value and ensured that I would supervise any schoolwork their teachers gave them. I happened to have those forms in my bag on the night I decided to try going to the cinema on my own for the very first time, after work one night that Andrew had the girls. I had chosen to watch a French movie at the cinema at Circular Quay. I treated myself with a big bag of chilli Copper Kettle chips and a glass of red wine. I was not really paying attention when the assistant told me the number of the cinema. I thought he had said Cinema Three. There was no ticket collector near the entrance to the cinema doors and each door was closed. I thought I must be late, so I quickly pulled the large door to Cinema Three open, letting in a shard of bright light. I tried not to draw further attention to myself as I moved down the stairs in the dark, carrying my red wine, bag of chilli chips, leather work bag and jacket. It seemed strange that the actors were speaking English, in a French film. The steps to the seats, which I couldn't see in the dark, were spaced differently to what I had anticipated, so my feet only found the edge of one step, not the actual step, and I toppled over, sending the red wine trickling over my dress and bag. It left a stain on the Department of Education papers requesting a formal leave of absence for my daughters from school and trying to represent myself as someone that could be trusted to be solely responsible for my children's education during the four weeks of school they would miss.

As soon as I found an empty seat, the movie ended. I had entered the wrong cinema, but I was too embarrassed to leave. I remained in my seat nursing a bleeding knee and a bruised ego and watched the next movie. I never saw the movie I originally went there to see. Despite the official papers being stained with red wine, the Department of Education did actually judge me fit to take my daughters out of school for four weeks of the school term.

*

We were on the early morning bus from Beauvais Airport, which is not in the centre of Paris. Beauvais is in fact nowhere, or in the middle of nowhere. It is where our discount airline flight dropped us. We were left with the choice of a €160 fare for a taxi or €17 for a bus to Porte Maillot, near the Arc de Triomphe, and from there catching the metro to the centre of Paris. We took the latter option, so getting to our hotel was still some time away.

Earlier that morning, we had caught the three am shuttle to the airport for a six am flight to Paris. The lack of sleep had seen Sonia and Olivia engage in an ugly public spat on the plane over who would have the window seat. I was stuck a few rows behind them, noticing not only their undignified behaviour, but also the knots in the scoop of their hoodies from lack of attention to their long hair. Requests for me to brush and braid their hair were coming less and less often. Sitting away from my daughters, I also noticed how they were changing. I had noticed for the first time the way the schoolboys at the airport looked at Sonia and the way Sonia looked at them. I also noticed that no one looked at me the way they did the last time I was in Europe, twenty or so years earlier, when my friend Jane and I were overwhelmed by the attention.

I decided to separate Sonia and Olivia for the bus ride into Paris, so as to avoid a repeat fight. Olivia sat next to me and Sonia sat behind me with an empty seat next to her. Olivia squelched a colourful squishy ball with concentrated vigour. It was a strange ball made of balloons with holes cut into it. It had been given to her by a hawker juggling on the street in Dubrovnik, who dared to pit his wit against hers and he lost. This meant he had to give her the ball. We weren't sure what was inside the ball that made it feel so squishy, but guessed by the way it felt that it was rice or wheat.

The grey sky offered only muted light during the trip. The rancid smell inside the bus suggested that someone on a previous trip had suffered motion sickness. I looked across the aisle to a couple sitting opposite us. Each was wearing a scarf as long as a python coiled around their neck. Instead of looking into each other's eyes, they looked in opposite directions, holding their luggage. As a single woman about to enter the world's most romantic city, this couple's lack of romance annoyed me. I felt that having a lover next to you and not paying them any attention was like the people I had just been sitting next to on the plane who had the window seat but instead of looking out the window, they closed the blind and went to sleep.

Outside the bus window were squared fields, the colour of Dijon mustard. I remembered looking down on these fields as I flew into Paris the first time as an independent twenty-three-year-old. I had wanderlust throughout university and worked for a few years afterwards to save enough money for a belated gap year to work in the UK and go travelling in Europe and South America. It was my first time overseas. Being from a family that had never left the country, and rarely crossed Sydney Harbour Bridge, I had no idea what to expect. So, when I arrived in Paris as my first stop, my backpack was already on the expanded setting, filled with a water purifier, electricity adapters, clothes for every season and fat guide books for places I may or may never have got to visit.

In the metro carriage en route to my hotel, my foot faltered and I found myself supine, on my backpack, legs in the air, like a turtle. My pack was so heavy I couldn't right myself, so Parisians needing to exit the carriage on their way to work, just walked over me.

I was determined that this entry into Paris with my daughters would not be an embarrassing disaster. Although I knew

I had reached the age of sensible shoe wearing, I was not allowing myself to wear runners or Birkenstocks. Olivia, who also instinctively knew the importance of a dress code, wore a T-shirt she had kept clean to wear as we entered Paris because it had 'French writing on it'.

I had taken my commitment to the Department of Education seriously. I genuinely wanted my daughters to gain a cultural appreciation and a hands-on study of European history, so, before our trip, weekends were spent prepping them. Before Chuppa Chup ate the television cord, we watched SBS documentaries and movies filmed in the countries we would visit. Much of this seemed to confuse, rather than elucidate. Olivia asked if Rome was in Romania and if Venice was in Venezuela.

We watched Sofia Coppola's movie, *Marie Antoinette*. The girls liked the pretty shoes and cakes. I liked the 1980s soundtrack: The Cure, New Order and Siouxsie and the Banshees. I tried to explain the history of the French Revolution, the growth of the middle class, new ideas percolating in coffee shops, the storming of the Bastille, and Marie Antoinette being decapitated. I was building momentum in the story to the announcement of the republic.

'Then the French citizens declared a…'

'Thumb war!' Olivia interjected loudly.

Sonia rolled her eyes and said in an exhausted voice, 'Mum, we just want to have *funness* on the holiday.' I realised then that I had Verbraekennised the holiday before we had even left the lounge room.

*

Rain beaded the window next to me and the tiniest of icicles formed around the window's edges between the rubber and the glass. Despite the cold day, the air conditioning in the bus seemed stuck on a refrigerator setting. Olivia had removed her hoodie but I could see that goose pimples were forming on her arms. I suggested she put her hoodie back on. She refused because she wanted everyone to see her T-shirt with the French writing. I moved closer, put my right arm around her and tried to warm her by rubbing her thin, suntanned arm. Instead of leaning in to me as expected, she stood and moved to the aisle of the bus, still kneading her squishy ball.

'Just 'cause you've got loner issues, doesn't mean you can hug me whenever you want!'

She then moved to the seat next to Sonia, who welcomed her as if *I* was their mutual enemy. I felt the eyes of the French citizens on the bus looking at me.

I remained staring at the space she had occupied as if my brain was trying to catch up. Then I realised I was staring into the eyes of the lovers across the aisle, who were staring back at me instead of at each other. So, I turned to face the window on my other side. I watched the mustard fields dissolve into graffiti-covered concrete as we drew closer to Paris.

After the sting lessened, I pulled my iPhone from my bag and began listening to music, letting the shuffle function choose the songs. Ordinarily, I was so vigilant for any potential danger surrounding my daughters that I never indulged in distractions. But at that moment, confined as we were, I decided to consciously ignore them and enjoy the novel experience of listening to music without a care in the world.

I noticed the random songs playing had a theme:

'*It's hard to believe that there's nobody out there, it's hard to believe that I'm all alone…*'

Shuffle.

'I've seen your flag on the Marble Arch and love is not a victory march, it's a cold and it's a broken hallelujah...'

The shuffle function was choosing loner songs!

'I'm like a waterlogged ball that no one wants to kick around anymore...'

Shuffle.

'Sexual healing, it's good for me...'

The problem with being a single mother – apart from not having anyone to slap sunscreen on your back, connect the two sides of the clasp on your necklace, hold side A while you slot in side B of IKEA's Borgsjö corner desk, share the decision-making, hold the ladder while you're replacing light bulbs, or have sex with – is that there is no other adult with whom you can share precious moments. It had taken many weekends without my children to stop worrying about them when they were at their father's and to learn to let go of what I couldn't control. I had learned to appreciate the solitude and independence of child-free weekends, but Olivia might have been right. I thought how nice it might be to be loved and to have someone who could say to me, 'Yes, you're doing a great job', or, 'You're so amazing, you take my breath away!' I fantasised about this as I scrolled through my iPhone to find my downloaded French lessons, which were introduced with a rousing blast of the *Marseillaise*, and I listened to them instead.

I had joined a salsa dancing class not long after returning to Australia, and I remembered now how challenging it had been to be touched again with a hand on my waist, or to be pulled in close and to feel another man's breath or sweat. I was also conscious of my 'mother body', my waistline and my belly so changed since the last time I was dating.

I did eventually start dating, but I found dating as a single mother was complicated. It didn't help that on one first date

Olivia had just become the mother of a Tamagotchi – a blue palm-sized virtual pet that needed nurturing to survive. Olivia hadn't wanted to take the Tamagotchi to her dad's house that night because she felt the pressure every new parent faces with a newborn, not knowing the difference between digital beeps to know if it wanted to be fed or toileted. Tamagotchis were an early experiment to see if humans could become emotionally attached to inanimate digital objects. I was a guinea pig in this experiment and at the same time, I had to determine if I could become emotionally attached to the man sitting opposite me. I nurtured Olivia's digital baby between courses while I tried to read the complex body language of this intriguing member of the opposite sex. It is often said that men are attractive to women if they are seen with dogs or children. This makes men look more caring. But for women to appear attractive to men, the advice is the opposite: women should appear to have no commitments to appear attractive to men. A digital baby could have blown the whole thing. As it turns out, he loved our digital baby and, as a single dad himself, he knew exactly what to do. We placed it on the table between us and took turns to feed and nurture it, discussing our baby Tamagotchi's likes and dislikes.

Still, I wasn't going to introduce my real daughters to this man until our baby Tamagotchi survived a little longer. We spent time together only on my childfree weekends, dining out and spending time on his boat, but then events took a turn. On one of those child-free weekends, as we were getting to know each other better in my living room, we were interrupted by several loud knocks at the front door. When I opened the door, Sonia and Olivia barrelled in. I had to quickly explain who the man in the living room was. I held their hands and guided them inside for introductions. That went well, then there was a painful silence. The girls stood in front of me, my arms around them both, as they twisted their bodies from side to side. They stared at something or nothing on the floor. Then Sonia remembered, 'Dad's waiting outside, we just came to get our swimmers for the pool.' They ran to their rooms and I met them again at the door to kiss them goodbye. I was bent down, balancing on the balls of my feet to hug Olivia at her height. Then she came in close to my face. Crestfallen, she asked, 'Does this mean we won't see Daddy anymore?'

*

We had reached the outskirts of Paris and I saw that they were no nicer than the outskirts of any other city. The bus was slowing and occasionally stopped in traffic. I took my earphones out and turned to advise Sonia and Olivia that we were getting closer to Paris. Sonia took out her earphones to hear what I had to say, and as she did, I noticed that Olivia had devised an alternative way to stay warm. Having rejected my hugs, and my suggestion to wear her hoodie, she had chosen to wear the thin blue socks from the complimentary toiletries bag she'd been given on the flight out of Sydney. Olivia had her hands in the feet of the socks, so the socks extended along her arms – sock gloves or glove socks – like a cardigan without its body. She continued to squish her ball in her sock hands and looked at me defiantly.

I shook my head and returned to my French lessons, '*Mon mari va arrive a tout moment*' (my husband will arrive any minute), only to be interrupted by Sonia tapping me on the shoulder. I turned to look through the gap in the seats. Olivia's arm socks were no longer blue but white. Her new T-shirt with the French writing was covered in a powder of white, as were her black leggings. I couldn't understand what had happened. I couldn't see the full picture from between the seat, so I stood up to face them. Olivia and Sonia, their clothes, their seats, and their backpacks were covered in a soft spray of what looked like baby powder. The two lovers across the aisle now looked like pizza dough, their clothes and luggage also splattered in white. They looked momentarily confused, then disgusted. Olivia's squishy ball had exploded. We knew conclusively now that it had been filled with flour. When Olivia's eyes met mine, she raised her eyebrows, tilted her head, shrugged her shoulders and mouthed the word, 'Sorry' as we approached the Arc de Triomphe.

At the Pantheon with the Obamas

In Rome, the heat stuck to our skin like dirt. The air-conditioned shops along the path to the Pantheon gave us some relief. I tried on dresses I couldn't afford in Luisa Spagnoli, where the shop assistants made it clear that I looked like I couldn't afford them. We were already exhausted from crowd-jamming through the Colosseum, so I added up the euros in my travel wallet and decided to splurge on a restaurant meal, instead of our usual pizza slice and gelato. The restaurant was full of tourists. A young wiry waiter promptly took our order. He returned and set plates and cutlery on the white linen tablecloth for four places, although there were only three of us. I was about to say something, but his brusque manner and broken English made me think better of it. Maybe they set every table for four.

About ten minutes later, the waiter was back. He delivered four plates of lasagne to the white linen and turned to leave.

'*Scusi*!' I said. The tourists at the surrounding tables turned to look. The waiter, however, did not.

'*Scusi*!' I repeated a bit louder.

The waiter returned and stood between Sonia and I: '*Si?*'
'You've given us four meals, but there are only three of us.'
'You order four!'
'No, I ordered three.'
'You order four!' He slammed his hand flat on the table, signalling an end to the discussion.

I saw my children's bodies stiffen. I took a breath and said in a calm voice, 'There are only three of us.' I opened my arms wide to show one daughter seated on each side of me as proof.

'You order four, you eat four, and you pay four.' He straightened his arms and pointed to the four plates of lasagne, imitating the gestures I had just made.

Tourists at the peripheral tables looked on, annoyed. We had been offered food that we would not eat. They, on the other hand, struggled to get the waiter's attention. The family next to us stopped eating and turned all four of their heads like nosey neighbours. It was true that all the tables around us had four diners. One father, one mother, two children. It was also true that our table did not.

The waiter stood with the bill in his hand, just behind my shoulder.

'Four lasagne, sixty euro.'

Sonia bowed her head towards the table and whispered, 'Mum, just pay for it.'

'It's not right!' Olivia challenged. 'There are only three of us!'

I remembered I only had €45.

'I only have money for three.'

I showed him the money and the emptiness of my wallet, and he half turned his back in disgust. I held the colourful notes out until he turned back around, snatched the money in one hand, lifted the fourth plate of lasagne with the other and stormed off aggressively, speaking in Italian to his fellow waiters.

'Single parent,' I heard the father seated at the table next to us say to his wife and children, as if no further explanation was needed. We ate quickly and left, despite needing to rest longer. We filled our drink bottles at the Fontana della Barcaccia at the base of the Spanish Steps, purposefully wetting our runners as we did so, and squelched loudly as we walked to the Pantheon with cooled feet.

*

Our spirits lifted as we entered the Pantheon's dark, marbled coolness. We sat down to rest, even though it was loud with tourists. Olivia and I sat on a wooden pew, looking up at the elaborate high dome, as Sonia bumped around taking photographs. We could hear tour guides talking about the open circle of sky at the centre of the dome, the oculus.

'It was once the eye to the heavens for all the Roman gods.'

The oculus reminded me of the skylight in the courthouse, when I sought protection from my former husband. I was grateful our lives had become more peaceful. However, it reminded me that before we left for our holiday, Andrew had shown that he still had the power to throw our lives into chaos. Despite signing for the passports and for the girls to travel, the week before we left, he informed me that he had decided to not allow the girls to travel after all. I was to find out in that week that he did indeed have the power to stop the girls leaving, even if he had given prior consent. The Family Court allows for a parent to raise an objection to their children going overseas and a tribunal appointed by the court needs to be convened to decide the case. This process takes a minimum of a week. If Andrew had done this, we would have missed our flights. As it turned out, he did not actually file an application, but I couldn't know for certain that we would actually be free to travel until we arrived at check-in. For this reason, I couldn't sleep the night before we left. At three am I had scanned the girls' passports on our printer, to have a copy for our eight-thirty am flight in case they were lost or stolen. When I reached check-in, though, I realised I had left the passports near the printer. I'd planned every detail of the trip. Now this. I just wanted to collapse at that point and for someone else to take over, but my daughters showed no sign of alarm. They just looked at me with such faith, as if they knew I would solve it. I called my friend and neighbour, Carol, who lived across the road and had a key to our house. She collected the passports but she needed to go to work, so she raced the passports to another friend, Fiona, who lived down the street. Fiona was on her way to work but made a detour to deliver the passports to the airport. It worked out, thanks to the kindness and quick actions of my friends. We missed a flight and we were without luggage for two days in Malaysia, but we had successfully left the country.

As we sat in the Pantheon, my eyes were drawn to the statue of Mary above Raphael's tomb, holding the baby Jesus. Travelling throughout Europe with my daughters, I had again seen the paintings and statues of Mary and Jesus that had so impacted me as a young woman. I connected with these images now as a divorced single mother in a completely different way. If one was ignorant of the religious significance, Mary and her baby, appeared like a single parent family. In the sculpture, baby Jesus is standing, stretching his legs against his mother, standing up as she holds him, helping him to balance. I smiled at the memory of my children at the same age pressing into the cellulite of my thighs with their little feet as they were impatient to stand.

My thoughts were interrupted when Olivia nestled her body into mine. The circle of light coming from the ceiling made me notice for the first time the patches of blue on her face and wonder what they were. It turned out that the dye from a cheap sarong purchased in Malaysia must have stippled her skin as she dribbled in her sleep, while using it as a blanket on the overnight train. Olivia and I hugged and laughed there in the circle of light coming from the oculus. Sonia snapped a photograph of us.

A Spanish tour group passed. I could translate short phrases: 'Built by Hadrian ... formed from two circles ... same height and width.' My daughters were impressed with my language skills. Then there was an announcement in Italian, which I thought was offering tours. My daughters were less impressed when we found out that it was actually an order to evacuate. Police officers entered and quickly cleared the building. Ordinarily I would have wanted to take my children well away from any risk. But, despite the heavy police presence, we didn't feel any danger. In fact, there was an atmosphere of fun and theatre. The police cordoned off the Piazza della Rotonda. They corralled us using yellow plastic tape emblazoned in blue with the words, *Polizia Municipale ROMA*. We gathered with the impromptu crowd outside, facing the Pantheon.

My daughters wouldn't let me try to ask what was happening in Italian, because they were embarrassed by my previous unsuccessful attempts. So, we just allowed ourselves to be swept up in the mystery. An arrogant German shepherd sniffed the square. The girls thought he was Rex the police dog, from the television show. They called out, 'Rex!' to get him to come closer for a pat. His handler was not amused. Then twenty police with the title *Polizia di Finanzia*, sped into the plaza on motorbikes under blue flashing lights. They parked in formation around the square. Then they left their bikes and stood facing the crowd. The *carabinieri* joined them, so that together they blocked our view. These young, tanned *carabinieri* only had to blow whistles to make people do what they required. They stood legs astride in tight-fitting pants, hands on their guns and truncheons. They looked impressive, but they were dwarfed by the silent, ancient columns of the Pantheon behind them, stretching to the cosmos.

The windows in the restaurants around the square were filled with both patrons and chefs. Above them, I noticed snipers paced the roofs, but I did not draw my children's attention to this. Around us, children sat high on father's shoulders. It was then that we picked up the word 'Obama'. Of course! President Obama was in Rome for the G8 meetings – the *G otto*, as the Italians called it.

A siren heralded the entry of the police inspector in a black car. Shorter and plumper than many of the younger *carabinieri*, he was a stereotype of an Italian detective. His shirt bloused loose over his jeans, buttons opened to expose a gold chain trapped in his chest hair, a cigarette hanging from his mouth. He had the look of a man who had freshly made pasta waiting for him at home each night. He strutted and yelled at the young police officers. An hour and a half passed without us noticing, so caught up in the spectacle were we.

Then a stylish black car arrived and parked at the entrance to the Pantheon. A woman in a yellow dress stepped out in full view. 'Michelle Obama! Look, it's Michelle Obama!' She waved generously and the crowd cheered and took photographs for a few minutes. The zoom lens on my camera was stretched to its max. She entered the Pantheon. The crowd twittered in every European and Asian language, shared photographs and called relatives. We had forgotten about the incident with the waiter, the heat and our sore feet, so intoxicated were we with our good fortune. To be at this place, at this time, to have Michelle Obama wave at us.

No one dispersed and about fifteen minutes later an oversized, bulletproof black car arrived. The crowd went silent. Cameras paused.

'Could it really be?'

'The President?'

'Barack Obama?'

No one left the car. Instead, Michelle Obama appeared from inside the Pantheon. But instead of wearing a yellow dress with her hair down, as we had seen her enter the Pantheon, she appeared in an elegant black dress with her hair in a fancy updo. Confusion fell upon the crowd. Her daughters, Sasha and Malia were with her, also in elegant dresses with their hair in fancy updos. They waved gracefully and the crowd again burst into cheers and bravos. My daughters were excited to see two girls so similar in ages to them. It was a very special moment. Michelle and her daughters, me and my daughters. How similar we were, I thought. Michelle is just two years older than myself; our girls are similar ages, all of us at the Pantheon in Rome doing the tourist thing. My mind drifted to how we might have had fun hanging out together if this crowd was not between us, two mums with our daughters, perhaps trying on dresses in Luisa Spagnoli together. Then my daughters started asking questions and my daydream ended.

'Where did Michelle Obama change dresses?'

'How did Sasha and Malia arrive?'

'Was there an underground entrance?'

'Were they helicoptered in through the oculus?'

These questions remained unanswered when Michelle, Sasha and Malia were driven off in the large black car and disappeared. Then the woman dressed in yellow, who I had photographed in the belief that it was Michelle Obama, left the Pantheon without fanfare. She strolled down the street, talking on a walkie-talkie, and turned the corner. The crowd's emotions flatlined. Then Sonia and Olivia wanted me to ask someone in Italian what was going on. Was the woman we had first thought was Michelle Obama merely a decoy? Was she a security guard? We were confused about what we had just witnessed, and what we had been part of.

Working through it, I realised we had given up time at the Pantheon on the one and only day we could go there. We had spent two and a half hours of our European holiday standing in a plaza to watch and cheer a woman who may have been a security guard dressed as the American President's wife. I felt such a fool for my fantasy. The divide between Michelle, her daughters, and myself and my daughters suddenly became very clear to me.

Michelle Obama was a woman I admired, seeing her brought home for me how much my life had changed. Before my life took a different turn, I would have considered that I was on a path towards being a leader, contributing, even in a small way, to bringing about a more caring and just society. So much of my energy in the past ten years had been spent fighting for justice, for protection, for rights, for freedoms, not for others, just for my children and myself – I had no longer had the energy to do this in a professional capacity for anyone else.

At that moment, I saw us as the shop assistants in Luisa Spagnoli had seen us when I asked to try on a dress. I saw their gaze go to our feet to look at the three of us from our shoes up. Our socks displayed ingrained patterns of dirt, stiffened from being washed only with hotel soap in hotel basins. The girls' legs were mottled with mosquito bites acquired at a midnight solstice festival on a beach in Pitrags with our friends in Latvia. Some of these bites had been scratched ceaselessly during our stay in Dubrovnik, turning them into angry sores. Some of us had chronic body odour, no doubt resulting from certain clothes being favoured more than others, namely a T-shirt fronted with the statement, 'Some of us are just born cool', worn by a daughter who sometimes acted as though she believed it. Another daughter was sporting an injury on her chin acquired and stitched together in Malaysia. Olivia also still had some random blue dye patches on her face from the sarong.

Just like the Michelle Obama decoy, so many things that had appeared one way now appeared completely as another. Scenes from my life played out in my head, but not the way I had originally seen them. I had been the protagonist in a play who had been offstage when the audience was made privy to the real drama and I was just catching up.

I realised that when Andrew moved to Sydney and into my house, it wasn't the act of commitment I had understood it to be. The reason for his move was that he had lost his job, but he had presented the situation as giving up his job for his love for me. It made me feel special and it made me feel obliged to support him and let him stay at my house and give a level of commitment I might not have given so early in a relationship otherwise. The first manipulation was clear now. I saw, too, how being told I was 'too sensitive' as a child when my brother punched me seemingly for the fun of it, gave me an early message that I had to accept such things, and if I didn't, there was something wrong with me. I began to see the incessant teasing by my father, brother and brother-in-law when I was at university was done to ensure I didn't forget my place. That's when I realised this wasn't about me, or my children, or my dad, or Andrew. That's when I realised the whole situation was unworkable.

I saw how the mother track of work that wound around the needs of family was an uneven, lonely and makeshift path. It was not part of some innovative gig economy. The years of casual work from home and part-time work had been the disintegration of a career, not the continuation of one. My labour plugged gaps in the workforce, but I was not seriously considered part of it. Each time I re-entered in a full-time role, I entered at a lower level than where I had left before becoming a mother. At interviews for the jobs that were at the level I knew I could work best, they asked limiting questions, 'What have you done in your last job that is similar to this job?', rather than asking what I was capable of or giving me a hypothetical challenge to show it. The rest of my years spent being a mother was seen as the doing of nothing. Not recognised or rewarded but given full responsibility for the outcomes and judged if things didn't always go according to plan.

*

Police cars and bikes sped off. The excitement in the square dissipated. Space opened as the crowd thinned. As if by instinct, my daughters ran forward with the other children in the piazza, snapping the *Polizia Municipale ROMA* tape that had separated myself and the First Lady. Long yellow streamers of it took off on the breeze into the afternoon sky. I imagined a slice of plastic tape reaching the top of the Pantheon and making its way through the oculus to land for the amusement of Mary and Jesus in front of Raphael's tomb. Sonia and Olivia ran through the piazza, flying kites of tape behind them. Working as a team, they successfully competed with boys from around the world to collect the largest batch in their arms and curl them into bundles. It reminded me of my sister and I as suburban pirates finding furniture from junk piles. The girls threw the scraps of tape up in the air and let it rain on them like cartoon millionaires showering themselves with money, but were quick to grab it again before the boys did. They skipped with long ropes of the stuff. Eventually, I called them over to leave. They stuffed some of the tape into their backpacks as a souvenir. Then we walked in the direction of Fontana di Trevi to get some gelato and throw coins in the fountain.

'Mum, do you think Malia and Sasha got some of the tape?'

'No, they didn't get to come out and play like you did.'

*

That night, when I should have been cooking dinner in our apartment, I was instead sprawled on the bed face down, like a victim in a crime scene. We were on our trip, we shouldn't have had a care in the world, but somehow the morning's incident with the waiter and the shop assistants and Michelle Obama's decoy had left me feeling that I had nothing to believe in. Sonia and Olivia sat on the bed next to me, gently poking or softly tickling along my side, trying to ignite sparks of fun. They sat on my back and began to brush my hair. This was soothing, but they ensured there would be no dozing off or feeling sorry for myself. One daughter would occasionally ask softly in one ear if I was enjoying it, then the other would yell to her sister that it was now her turn to brush. Eventually, they pulled my arms backward and I had to surrender to their demand to sit upright in a chair, so they could work each side of my long hair into an updo. Sonia stood in front of me and parted my thick hair using her fingers, then moved behind me and handed half the heavy bundle to Olivia. Then there was pulling and itching and crimping as they competed for the most outrageous updo on each half of my head with my long hair. Excited by the challenge, they chatted and giggled a bit too close to my ears. We only had a few hair bands, so they had to make do, zigzagging the hair back into itself in creative ways. They formed lots of thin ponytails, then braided them, leaving some splayed at different angles and others pulled into a bun. They walked me to the mirror, hung on a wall painted with frescos, to face myself. I saw that some hair had been aerated in high 'cassowary lumps', as they called them. The rest was a dog's breakfast.

'Look, Mum! You're beautiful – just like Michelle Obama.'

Shifting

When Olivia started high school, everything shifted. The last of the pencil marks climbing the wall in our kitchen had stopped at 'Sonia 92cm', although she was now almost as tall as I was. School timetables and excursion reminders had replaced the children's paintings that had brightened the fridge. It was only the fridge itself that remained immovable at the centre of a swirling magic that turned my daughters into teenagers, their childhood selves immortalised in photographs stuck to its door. There was no ritual or ceremony to mark the changing from compliant, beaming supporters who greeted me every morning and afternoon, to the complex moaning dissenters who tried to scuttle any plan I had for an easy life. It was only the consistent wearing of earphones and eyes downturned to mobile devices that marked the transformation.

Paraphernalia from their past was stored in the top of the wardrobe – school reports, 'Player of the Match' trophies, that always had a figurine of a boy kicking a ball, ribbons with numbers assessing the order of their achievement, Sonia's first pair of glasses, Olivia's first ballet shoes, cardigans knitted by my mother and booties knitted by aunties that still smelled of babies.

Unlike the record-keeping of earlier firsts – first tooth, first word, first walk – I wondered what should be recorded as 'firsts' for this new phase of their lives. First period? First Facebook post? First swear word? Should the 'lasts' be recorded? The last time we ate dinner without a mobile phone on the table. The last time we went shopping together. The last time I was called upon to help with homework. The girls now travelled to different high schools half an hour away. They were no longer afforded the connection with the local bush around them and the protection and support of our neighbourhood during the day. I no longer knew their friends, their friends' parents and siblings, their dogs and their walking habits. As tweens I had already taught both girls to assemble flat-packed furniture, carve a Halloween pumpkin, make omelettes, pancakes, nachos and spaghetti Bolognese, and set privacy settings on social media accounts. When I tried to teach Sonia how to surf, just buying the wax needed for her board exposed us to a range of inappropriate choices. There was Mr Zogs Sex Wax, Mr Zogs Pickle or Sticky Bumps and Mighty Mounds, shaped as women's breasts, or Mrs Palmer's Ultra Sticky, 'the best grip around'. It made me wonder if anything had changed at the beach, since the days of *Puberty Blues*.

Sonia and Olivia owned mobile phones, so they communicated directly with their father and caught public transport to their father's house from school. Interacting less with Andrew made my life more peaceful and the phones gave the girls more freedom to communicate when they wanted, the way they wanted.

I had taken Olivia's advice to address my 'loner issues'. I had said 'yes' instead of 'no' to requests for coffee with a single father of one of Olivia's primary school friends. His wife, a much-respected and generous woman from the school community, had died after a long illness.

He appeared in the playground each afternoon at school pick-up like an exclamation mark. He was tall and thin, towering above the children and other parents. Unlike the other dads in suits and ties, he wore jeans and a T-shirt. He walked with a swagger but talked softly and gesticulated with his hands as he spoke. His cheekbones and jawline were chiselled and he had an unapologetic nose. His head was topped with what the other mothers referred to as salt and pepper hair.

We often found ourselves near each other at basketball games or school concerts, both of us taking videos of our children's achievements, committed to capturing significant moments of our children's lives. Living in the same close-knit village meant chance interactions, such as shopping for fruit and vegetables, allowed our regard for one another to grow.

Eventually, we managed a weekend away from our children to spend time together in a sandstone cottage by the sea. In front of a warm fireplace, we were talking when emotion overtook him and I noticed his mouth become loose at its edges, like a child's first drawing of a circle. I moved in closer. He placed his heavy head on my chest as I slid lower on the couch and folded him in. I wasn't used to being called on in this way. I felt a liquid warmth rise through my body. I slowly stroked his hair, my fingers tracing its soft loops. He relaxed and his head became heavier. I tried to keep my breath even, to stop my chest rising, to give him a soft but stable pillow. To do this, I looked up at the patterned, pressed ceiling, painted white. It was a bountiful scene: garlands of grapes tied with ribbons, bowls of fruit pressed into each corner. The garlands looked real, as if the ribbons were flowing, the fruit appeared to have depth, the plump grapes looked like they could be eaten. The white paint was lifting at the edges, poised to fall on us like autumn leaves, as we laid bare our truths. But the paint didn't fall like leaves, the grapes were not eaten, the ribbons did not flow; they remained weightless above, as we became locked together below.

*

I realised I had fallen in love when I noticed hearts everywhere, instead of noticing couples everywhere. These hearts arrived in the shape of rocks in my garden, the shape of the petals on purple flowers randomly growing along my fence, in the shape of the chicken schnitzels Sonia and Olivia ordered when we ate out and even a bird poo delivered on my car window landed in the shape of a love heart.

It was a floaty, trippy love, not expected in one's forties. I've noticed that the only couples in their forties that show public displays of affection tend to be having affairs. Long-term, happily married couples rarely even hold hands in public. I assume our fellow Illawarra line commuters thought we were having an affair when we hugged on the train platform each morning as we saw each other on our way to work, then sat hand in hand on the morning express to the city.

We found in each other hidden pools of silliness that had for both of us been left stagnant for a long time. We were more like teenagers than our actual teenage daughters. We giggled and splashed in those cool refreshing pools as if it was the long school summer holiday, so much so that I stopped the habit of continually checking for approaching storms – so I did not anticipate the one that was brewing.

Teenagers Tear at One's Bowel

In the year Australia's first female prime minister, Julia Gillard gave her famous speech about misogyny in parliament, she made reference to the leader of the opposition, Tony Abbott, having said in an interview that he did not see the lack of representation of women in higher office in Australia as a problem because he believed men were physiologically and psychologically more suited to command.

*

That same year, in my twenty-fifth year as a social worker, my fifteenth year as a mother and my fifth year employed to write parenting publications, Olivia made it clear to me that, in her opinion, I knew nothing about children, being a mother, or anything. It was during this time the words written by VS Pritchett, 'children tear at one's bowels', resonated most painfully with me.

I was gathering Olivia's still-perfumed clothes off the floor in her room to wash when something caught my eye on her 'smiling wall' which had grown from ten photos to cover the wall over the past six years. It sat in the section of older photos, below a photo of Daylight and Midnight when they were pups. It was above a photo of her receiving a gymnastics award, where her smile looks stretched beyond the natural perimeter of her mouth by a hair bun I might have made too tight to prevent it falling out while she was upside down. It was bordered on one side by a snapshot of Dumper, Thumper and Yawning Jumper, who were no longer with us; and on the other by Olivia and Sonia in the backyard, suspended in flannelette pyjamas from the tyre swing. There was the photo of all of us holding on tight at Splash Mountain in Disneyland and a photo of the four of us and a snowman in Lake Tahoe.

The photo that usually held the position amongst these was one of my favourites. It had been taken at Olivia's preschool when we lived in Los Angeles. Olivia and I were dressed as witches for our first American Halloween. Not just any witches; we were mermaid witches. The photo captures us cuddling and laughing as Olivia sits on my lap in a sea of bubbly crepe paper surrounded by smiling jellyfish. A scrap of notepaper filled the space where the photo had been and part of the Halloween photo was stuck onto it, the part of me dressed as a witch – alone. Olivia had cut me out. She'd detached herself from me. The fish and the sea were also missing. She'd blackened my teeth and thickened my eyebrows with black pen. It was shocking. At the same time, it reminded me of something I had seen before. I remembered then, the girls and I had watched the news only a few nights before when the federal opposition leader had stood in front of placards that depicted Australia's first female prime minister as a witch. When my daughters saw this, they informed me that their father also had a picture of an evil witch that appeared when my mobile number rang his phone.

The placards the opposition leader stood in front of read 'Ditch the Witch' and described the prime minister as a 'Bitch'. Similarly, above my black pointy hat, written in black pointy letters, was a word that had been written on placards about the prime minister, a word Andrew used to call me, a word that rhymed with witch. I sank onto her bed, clutching her dirty clothes. I didn't understand what was happening, but I sensed that this was beyond *The Magic Bellybutton Girl* to fix.

I remembered when 'poopooweeweeheadie' was the most harmful insult Olivia could summon. Now she had assembled a language arsenal and fired it with nuclear precision. It threw me off my course of confident parenting. It penetrated the fibro sheeting of our house and ricocheted down the street. Neighbours made it clear that they had heard these shots fired randomly throughout the day or night. Missiles could be triggered in shopping centres or other public places for maximum impact. I made it clear that it was not acceptable for her to speak to me like that. It made no difference. She continued to drop obscenities like the rap artists I could hear escaping through the barrier of her headphones.

'Are you friggin' kidding me... They're earphones not headphones.'

Earphones or headphones, whichever she was wearing, were sometimes a blessing for both of us. But living in the same house and being of the same flesh and blood meant we sometimes needed to actually communicate.

Touch had always been Olivia's language – more immediate and more accurate than words. When she was younger, she preferred to sit on my lap and observe others playing, whereas Sonia would run off to be with others at the first chance. As a toddler, Olivia would slip her hand into mine when we walked. We'd cuddle up together on the lounge to watch movies and she'd loved me brushing and braiding her hair, it relaxed her so much that she often fell asleep on me when I did so. But in the year she began high school, Olivia's hugs became so rare that the imprint of her touch stayed on my skin the way an exquisite meal stays on the palate.

I couldn't catch up with what was happening. I had expected that the teenage years would involve some changes to my previous positions as observer, recorder, supporter, decision-maker and comforter. I knew that Olivia would take on some of these roles herself and some roles might be given to others – but I expected this to happen over time and with negotiation, not as a strident, violent cut. She was asserting her independence as I had once done with my own parents. I understood the idea that self-expression, as well as some defiance, is necessary for children to develop into healthy adults, and the idea that teenagers will express their unpleasant feelings to the ones they know will still love them after hearing it. Nevertheless, I felt the pain of it, just as my parents must have once felt it.

Adrienne Rich, in her book *Of Woman Born*, wrote of the 'flow of energy between two biologically alike bodies'. When one had spent nine months inside the other, it creates the materials 'for the deepest mutuality and the most painful estrangement'.

I swotted evidence-informed strategies that were proven to support adolescents through this turbulent time and tried to follow these.

'Adapt to meet her changing needs.'

I tried to find out her new needs, without getting in her way. I moved through the house as if it were dotted with land mines. Despite my carefully strategised peacekeeping operations, I sometimes blundered. Such as the time I came to the door to collect Olivia from a party, instead of waiting in the car, or when I wore a dress she didn't like to a school function. I also spoke to a teacher without her permission, and I friended a friend's mother on Facebook without her prior consent.

'Have family dinners together at a table; routine is important.'

I offered the limited range of dishes that I knew would be pleasing, and we enjoyed eating fish, chips and salad down by the river on Monday nights during summer.

'Consistency and boundaries are important.'

My daughters had to navigate living in two homes with two different sets of rules every week. I was consistently amazed at how well they handled that. Then in high school Olivia twigged on to the advantages of such an arrangement. If Olivia hadn't done her homework, Andrew texted the school, 'Olivia left her books at her mother's house.' If Olivia didn't want to wear her school socks, he'd text, 'I think Olivia's school socks are in the washing pile, hehehe!' Setting limits or consequences was impossible, so, despite promoting evidence-based authoritative parenting strategies in my profession, my ability to follow any such strategy at home was continually challenged. 'I'll go and live at Dad's house' was all Olivia needed to say to get what she wanted from me too.

I understood that teens often misread adult facial expressions as anger – perhaps that explained our interactions at the time – meeting perceived anger with anger. Either way, Andrew seized upon the discord. If I said no, Andrew said yes. When Olivia lost interest in school and her grades dropped, I was the only parent called into the year adviser's office to account for it.

I approached services for support, and they insisted that both parents had to be involved. Andrew did not acknowledge there was a problem. Instead, my new partner and I decided to attend a course about parenting teenagers together, given that between us we had four teenagers. In the parenting group there was a mix of married couples, single mothers and step-parents. The presenters, talking from their own experience as a long-term happily married couple had no suggestions for how to work their simple idea of applying consistent rules in one household across different family configurations.

Perhaps Olivia saw me as Verbraekennising her life. I had valued education because it had not been valued for me. Olivia was incredibly intelligent and a deep thinker, as was Sonia, but an education that involved sitting down and being told what to do was the last thing on Olivia's mind. I had felt I had to battle my parents' expectations of me as a teenager, just as Olivia was now making clear that she was not put on this earth to fulfil my expectations of her.

Olivia no longer allowed me to brush her knotty hair, but she still allowed me to occasionally braid it, particularly during exam times. This might have helped to calm exam nerves, and she also noticed that the girls with French braids received higher grades. On that morning I wasn't given much notice that braids were needed before leaving for work. French braids were more complicated than the braiding from my grandmother's days. Nevertheless, I deliberately tried to take longer to braid it than necessary. She sat on the white leather ottoman between my bent legs, as I sat on the lounge behind her. There was a damp electricity between us when I started. I softly and purposefully gathered just the top section of her hair into three equal-sized bunches. I gently smoothed it to avoid 'cassowary lumps'. Then I knitted small sections of hair left out to join the three bunches of hair, from one side and then the other. I was nervous about getting the pattern on each side exactly the same; this was always difficult. I leaned against her and could feel her fast heartbeat throughout her body. I thought through the conversations I wanted to start. I wanted to know what was making her feel so angry and to offer her reassurance. I tried to relay this intention through my fingers as she sat in silence. Just having the words in my head was enough to slow my breath. I worked in silence, brushing, flattening, folding, I slowed my movements to match my slowing breath. Then her breath joined my rhythm.

I reminisced about the slow, early days of wonder-watching, when I'd had to take the time to watch and learn who each of my children were and to understand their unique way of communicating what they needed. Perhaps I needed to again see my daughter as an unknown intelligent being, that had just landed on earth for me to care for, as I'd had to when she was born. To be fascinated with her behaviour, to watch her as she explored her world with new challenges, to get to know her as she now was, her new likes, her new dislikes, her new relationships, without judgement.

I had found over the years that the problem with parenting at every stage is that you never know what it is that you don't know. It was always my children who made me aware of what it was I didn't know. They were charging ahead with their own development, stepping into a new circle of security they were creating for themselves, and I again felt I was running behind in their wake.

I tried focusing on the positive behaviours, hoping this would shift the mood in the house. That is the gold standard of advice given to parents to help them during the teenage years.

'Catch your adolescent doing good things and praise that.'

With the tight-wired attention of a cat stalking a bird, I watched and I waited... and waited... and waited...

*

Giulia Giuffrè describes the invisible bindings of motherhood as bonsai wires. She writes, 'As life-changing for the mother as the birth itself is the daily experience of looking after children. Not so dramatic, but relentlessly transformative. Bonsai wire, not secateurs.'

Epilogue

A change of government had divided the nation into lifters or leaners. In this simple dichotomy, lifters in the view of the government, were people who worked and leaners were people who didn't. Women who undertook paid work were seen as lifting the country, but when women did the unpaid work of looking after their elderly or sick relatives, or their children, they were leaners. At the same time, the Australian Bureau of Statistics estimated the value of unpaid care work to the economy to be 43 per cent of the value of gross domestic product, equivalent to $434 billion. It is overwhelmingly women doing this work. But this caring work is not included in the economic figures, it remains invisible and therefore makes it easy for those not doing unpaid care work to consider it the doing of nothing.

The treasurer who made this statement about lifters and leaners was found to have taken a family holiday to Singapore without paying for it, claiming as a defence that he didn't realise he hadn't paid for it.

I was standing in the doorway in my work clothes saying goodbye to Sonia as she left for her first day at university.

She was overwhelmingly positive and couldn't wait to throw herself into university life. She was invincible. As she passed down the driveway, she stopped to pull out a large envelope from the letterbox and brought it to me. The familiar coat of arms showed it was from the federal government. Instead of a passport, or a child support letter, it was a bowel cancer prevention kit that instructed me to offer up my poo for bowel cancer screening.

Just as I had not been prepared for those intensive, earlier years of motherhood, I had not prepared for the changes that would come after them. The end of Sonia's schooling took me by surprise. So much effort had been focused on achieving a high mark in the final exams at her selective school that I couldn't believe her formal education had ended. There was still so much of life she needed to know.

After Sonia could no longer be seen past my next-door neighbour's hedge, I remained in the doorway, looking out at the mature plants in the garden. I breathed in the scent of the English lavender my mother had planted, as it swept through the opened door. Rainbow lorikeets frolicked in the grevillea that Linda had given us. The sweet-smelling frangipani that Georgette had helped me plant years before was in full bloom.

I too was at university that year completing a doctorate. I too was embarking on a new challenge. Eighteen years after being offered a spot in an executive training program, which I didn't accept at the time because I was pregnant, I was about to start my first role as an executive. I too couldn't wait to throw myself into it.

*

Olivia appeared from her bedroom, dressed and ready for school, her hair was brushed clean of knots. She stood next to me in the doorway, but didn't pass me to leave, as I had expected. She thumped her back pack, heavy with her laptop and textbooks, to the floor. She positioned herself slightly in front of me so that we were both facing the garden, and she looked where I was looking, as if to see my view.

The previous week, I had been driving Olivia to either her football game, or gymnastics or a party, I can't recall which one, when she had leaned across the gear stick that separated us and had used her whole hand like a brush, gently stroking my hair, with her other hand underneath. She had seemed intent on exploring the texture of my hair as if it were a drape of delicate fabric. I hadn't reacted. I had said nothing. I had just kept driving.

Olivia and I remained looking at the flowing movement of the tall, soft lavender stalks in the breeze. She subtly leaned her back against the front of my body, the way some people nonchalantly press into the front of a queue at a festival, instead of joining the back of the line. Her body gently fitted against mine – the missing puzzle piece. I had to stop myself from saying the things I wanted to say. I had to remain still, to not compromise that moment. I noticed she had grown taller; the top of her head fitted just under my chin. Her back had widened; I expected hardness, but she was softness. The weight of her body pressed even more against mine. That's when I realised she was allowing me to support her. When it seemed safe, I breathed out. I softened and slowly circled my arms around her, loosely at first, but my arms eventually found a resting place. This shift meant we were dependent on each other to remain balanced and upright. We stood this way in silence.

Author's Note

This book has been years in the making. It is a creative and literary rendering of a chapter from my life, but it is not the whole story of my life.

Writing this book has made the inherent risks and the ethical issues of autobiographical writing from a mother's perspective tangible. I am conscious that although this book is my story, it is also the story of others. During the writing and publishing process, I found the very potential risk of hurting anyone, let alone the people I care deeply about, overwhelming. At the same time, I feel strongly that this story and others like it are important to write and publish.

In writing and publishing the book I have tried to walk an ethical path, and to be as fair in my writing as possible. I waited until both my children are adults before making this book available. I have been mindful to de-identify individuals by changing names, dates and details. I have tried to present people in a balanced way by showing both their strengths and vulnerabilities and I have sought approval and permission to share the story from some who feature in it.

Author's Note

It is somewhat naïve to think that what happens in families stays in families. Particularly, where there has been abuse or a divorce, a family's previously private story is made public and examined by the judicial and social welfare systems, and discussed at length by neighbours, friends and family.

I am driven by a belief in the power of storytelling and the belief that stories written by mothers about the lives of mothers and children belong in the literary canon. Because this has not always been the case, some subject matter may be uncomfortable and this will necessarily be explored along with the love and joy of mothering. Not telling this story, however, would only add to the silence around important issues that impact families, and it is this silence that has already brought harm to women and children.

*

If something in this story has upset you, or you find there are similarities to your own story, you can talk to someone.

In Australia you can call 1800RESPECT, that is 1800 737 732, or Lifeline 13 11 14. These services are available 24 hours to offer support.

Acknowledgements

It's a cliché, but it does take a village to raise a child. Similarly, it has taken a village of wonderful people to help create this book. My sincerest gratitude to each and every one of them.

I would not have started writing *Binding* without Fiona Crawford's kindness and support in every way.

This book would not have been completed without the brave Dr Rachel Morley, who believed in this work and guided me with such patience and commitment to complete it as part of a Doctorate of Creative Arts. I extend my heartfelt thanks to her and co-supervisors Professor Matt McGuire and Dr Milissa Deitz. I am grateful to all the staff and students at the Writing and Society Research Centre at Western Sydney University where I completed my Doctorate of Creative Arts. I am also grateful to Professor Gail Jones for her mentoring. I also want to thank Professor Kate Douglas at Flinders University for her support.

An amended chapter from this book, was published in Griffith Review 51: Fixing the System (2016). I would like to acknowledge and thank *Griffith Review* for publishing this and for nominating my work for the US Pushcart Prize and Our Watch Award administered by the Walkley Foundation.

I was privileged to spend two weeks of uninterrupted writing time at Varuna Writer's Centre, where each night I could connect with and be inspired by accomplished writers around the dinner table. Thank you to the writers I spent time with at Varuna, in particular Emily Bitto and Julienne van Loon. One week at Varuna was sponsored by *Griffith Review* and the other by the Writing and Society Research Centre at Western Sydney University.

I am grateful to my fellow writers, particularly Jade Maloney, Dawn Adams, Fiona Wright, Jen Craig, Katie Sutherland and Miro Bilbrough for sharing their writing passion.

Thanks to Kim Swivel and Gina Flaxman for editing and proof reading, and for their kind words.

I can never thank enough my circle of friends who have been there for me and my family over many years. Especially Cristina, Nicola, Rob, Bernie, Carole, Fil, Louise, Linda, Petula, Alan, Stella, Geraldine, Mandy, Helle, Kristine, Karlis, Marlene, Tom, Althea, Kelly, Auna and the book club members.

Of course, I could not have completed this work without the support of my family. Thank you to my mum for all your love and care always. Thank you especially to my wonderful daughters. Thank you for your love and trust in me to share this story in the hope that it will help others.

www.ingramcontent.com/pod-product-compliance
Lightning Source LLC
Chambersburg PA
CBHW021430080526
44588CB00009B/486